Cornelius Walker

Outlines of Christian theology

Cornelius Walker

Outlines of Christian theology

ISBN/EAN: 9783337263638

Printed in Europe, USA, Canada, Australia, Japan

Cover: Foto ©Lupo / pixelio.de

More available books at **www.hansebooks.com**

OUTLINES

OF

CHRISTIAN THEOLOGY

BY

Rev. CORNELIUS WALKER, D.D.

Professor of Systematic Divinity in the Theological Seminary of Virginia

NEW YORK
THOMAS WHITTAKER
2 AND 3 Bible House
1894

CONTENTS.

CHAPTER	PAGE
I. Theology and Religion,	1
II. Sources of Theological Truth,	11
III. Canon of Scripture: That of Old Testament,	19
IV. Canon of Scripture: That of New Testament,	26
V. Inspiration of Scripture,	34
VI. Tradition, Mystery, Miracles,	61
VII. The Doctrine of God,	74
VIII. The Divine Attributes,	87
IX. The Doctrine of Trinity,	113
X. Creation and Origin of the World,	123
XI. The Doctrine of Man,	135
XII. The Doctrine of Sin,	149
XIII. Actual Sin,	160
XIV. Sin in its Consequences,	166
XV. Salvation from Sin,	176
XVI. Efficacy of Christ's Sufferings,	184
XVII. The Atoning Mediation,	197
XVIII. Christ's Work in its Application,	202
XIX. The Blessed Spirit in the Work of Salvation,	209
XX. The Church and Sacraments,	219
XXI. Angelology,	237
XXII. Eschatology,	245

PREFACE.

The object sought in the pages following is to present in brief outline the leading topics in a course of theological study. It is substantially that which the writer has pursued with his classes successively during the last eighteen or twenty years. The ultimate authority, as also the source of material, is that of inspired Scripture. For full statement and investigation of many of the subjects discussed, his pupils will recognize the text-book used—Knapp's "Theology"—as also others referred to—those of Dr. Hodge, of Hill, of Dorner, of Martensen, of Lindsay Alexander, and of Von Oosterzee. To these may be added, of more recent date, those of Dr. Buel, of Dr. Shedd, of Dr. Strong, and of Dr. Hodge, the younger. To the earnest student there is, in these works and others easily accessible, abundant material for full and thorough investigation of every issue and topic in Christian theology.

But while thus with the advanced student, the object here is to take hold of and to help the beginner, to indicate the substance and natural order of the problems with which he is called to deal, as also their grounds of evidence and verification. At the same time it is to be noted that the interest in these topics is not confined to this class—the theological student or candidate for the ministry. It extends to a much larger class—intelligent Christian readers, theologians to a certain degree of all classes. These have their rational interest in all the topics here presented. As mere technicalities, so far as possible, have been avoided, the objection in this respect to the ordinary reader has been removed. In all cases, moreover, of quotations of the original Greek and Hebrew, the English equivalent is annexed, so as to avoid all difficulty and obscurity. With the earnest prayer that it may do its work in the service of Him to whom it is offered, it is commended to its readers.

Outlines of Christian Theology.

CHAPTER I.

THEOLOGY AND RELIGION.

Theology, wherein a science.—Its sources of material, natural and revealed, and some of its forms of investigation and exhibition.—How religion different.—Some of the modes in which in the New Testament it is described.—What the science of religion.—Relation of theological and religious to other sciences.—Their apparent conflicts and how originating.—Wherein the philosophy of these different from their science.

THEOLOGY, in its name, claims to be a science. At one time, it was the almost only acknowledged science. If we bear in mind what is meant by this word, we shall see the propriety here of its application. Science is knowledge certified, as to its material; this material finding its systemization, and unifying principle or principles, in certain laws or modes of sequence, invariably operative. The positivist and the agnostic deny that there is any such knowledge as to God, either in the world or in specific revelation. But to the theist such position is irrational. If there be an Author of nature, capable of originating and sustaining nature, He will be capable also of making Himself manifest. Theology has to do with the nature and extent of such manifestation. It first asks, What do we find in this world of nature? Is nature a chaos or a cosmos? Do we find in this world of inorganic and organic being, relations, and connections, and dependencies? Do we find the presence and operation of law; relations of parts of the cosmos to each other, as to our capacity of comprehension? How do these make known their Author? Inductive processes properly come in here; are strictly scientific; as thus scientific, are properly theological.

So, too, with theology, science of God with additional material: the truths of natural manifestation, $\varphi\alpha\nu\varepsilon\rho\omega\sigma\iota\varsigma$, added to and made clearer in $\alpha\pi o\varkappa\alpha\lambda\upsilon\psi\iota\varsigma$, those of specific revelation. Given or accepting the fact of Divine Authorship of nature, no objection can be urged against the assertion of such revelation; and there are many features, in the manifestation of nature, that seem both to promise and demand it. The question, however, is one of fact; to be decided in view of the character of the evidence. The work of the theologian is to examine this evidence and the material which it brings to his knowledge; to find out what this manifestation of nature and what this word of revelation mean; and, through them, the character and will of their Divine Author.

This, of course, involves interpretation, arrangement, recognition of controlling and subordinate principles, distinction of facts and laws, laws from higher regulative principles, systemization, unification. As with all other sciences, this is the task of theology, the science of God.

As to the aspects under which this material may be investigated and studied, we may briefly indicate them. Biblical theology, for instance—a new term, or at least an old term with a new significance—is that which is arranged in the order of historical progress; truth about God, manifesting Himself, in the primæval, in the patriarchal, the Mosaic, the prophetic, the New Testament revelations. Systematic theology has in view the unification of all this material; to find in it not only progress and development, but a combined whole—a whole, in each one of its parts, as in their organic unity, manifesting the character and purpose of their Divine Author. This includes not only the clear statement of these truths, but their relations of connection and dependence. Historical theology, again, has in view the progress of thought and discussion, through which such statements have reached their present form, and been agreed upon; polemic, the statement of this truth, as related to errors of professed believers; apologetic, as related to difficulties made by unbelievers; and, last of all, practical theology, the effort to find practical application in these truths to the heart and life, whether in their systematic or unsystematic form. In all we are dealing with the same material: the truth of God, truth about God; the science, not the perfect, but the real knowledge of God, as He is, and as He stands revealed and related to His creatures.

In this respect, there is a difference with religion. "Religio," from *relego*, "scrupulous service to God," with Cicero; or "religio," from *religo*, "binding us to God," with Lactantius; or, in monastic idea, *relictus*, from *relinquo*, "leaving the world," is not so much a science as a practice. As with all forms of practice, religion may have its science; but this is not its essential nature. It is a knowing; but, in such knowing, also feeling and doing. As man, in his rational nature, is related to God, seeks after Him, that he may find Him, so the truths of theology teach him to exercise his capacity aright. In such exercise is religion: the subjective appropriation, in the mind and heart, and the working out in the life, of divinely given truth. This word religion, in ordinary usage, has more than one meaning, and we need distinguish them. A man's religion, for instance, or that of a community, is that of his accepted system of belief— in this sense really the equivalent of his theology. So again, it may, and does sometimes mean, the outward form, the ritual and worship, of such individual or community—their ecclesiastical system. These may be accompaniments. But there must be something else: the knowing, and feeling, and doing, as to God, and as obeying the will of God.

The degrees in which these terms are applicable, in the diverse conditions of men, are varied and manifold. And yet, with all, the lowest as the highest, we find the essential elements: truth as to God, theology; the spiritual nature of man, feeling after, and using such truth, religion. Whatever else may be said of human nature, it is religious! "There is no trouble," Dr. Sparrow used to say, "about men having religion of some kind or other; the trouble is to get them to have the right kind of religion." Such religious nature, in its working, endeavors to have a theology. Wardlaw alludes to the definitions "religion, theology subjectified; theology, religion objectified." While not fully exhaustive, it exhibits their main characteristics.

The New Testament names of religion have their significance. φοβος του Θεου, "the fear of Jehovah," of the Old Testament, is the fear of reverence, dreading the Divine disapproval, dreading the course leading to it; σοφια, the "wisdom" of the Old Testament, which finds the doing of God's will and service not only the way of right, but that of wisdom and welfare; δουλεια, the service of submissive obedience, which finds in the Divine law its rule of affection, as of action; λατρεια, the service not only of unreserved obedience, but of grateful adoration; ευλαβεια, the careful service, which finds in small as in great things exercise of the spirit of devotion; θρησκεια, such service finding outward expression, especially as it brings us in contact with the needs of our fellow-creatures; ευσεβεια, having the inward spirit, which gives value and character to everything else; and, last of all, οδος, "the way," and πιστις, "the faith," in which all these forms of action are quickened in the truths of the revelation of Jesus Christ.

But, as already intimated, while religion, in its essential nature, is a service, not a science, there is or may be a science of religion. In it, for instance, there are diversities of facts and manifestations, controlling laws and operations, a unifying principle with which they are all connected. The science of religion deals with these: the religious nature, the fact that man has such a nature, that he is consciously and manifestly related to a Higher Being, the object of his thoughts, his fears, his hopes, his aspirations. To trace out the workings of this nature, the operation of its principles, as exhibited in the individual, in the different religions of the world, and as modified by different conceptions of Deity—the occasions of any such system finding origin—its reactive influence upon its votaries—all this becomes the task of the scientist of religion. Religions may thus be classified. Some may be manifested as local, and incapable of expansion from their original centre; others, of wider range, but still limited to certain conditions of climate, social or moral advancement; others still wider, but, in their general result, morally and socially deteriorative—one claiming to be a world religion, actually controlling the highest form of moral and social civilization, and beneficial in its influence, as coming in contact with and displacing others. Evidently, in dealing with the material thus indicated, and the questions suggested, we are in the domain of science.

And this brings up an issue, at the present moment, of special interest, in connection with this subject:

the relation, as it is usually put, of theology, as of religion, to science ; more properly, the relation of theological and religious to physical, chemical, biological, mental, or moral science. That relation, ideally, is one of perfect harmony, touching at times, and at different points, the same material ; but in these different relations, parts of the same material, of one great whole. If we could have a perfect theology, many of the existing difficulties and conflicts would disappear. But not entirely. To secure that there must not only be a perfect theology, but a perfect geology, or chemistry, or biology, or whatever the science with which such conflict has been waged. As they are all actually imperfect, they are all liable to come in such conflict.

Such conflict, from the non-theological side, has usually come from one of two sources : so-called scientific results unverified ; so-called scientific results of what really belongs, not to science, but to philosophy. From the theological side, such conflict comes sometimes from the misapplication of theological truth to matters with which it has no concern ; sometimes, and much more frequently, from adherence to accepted scientific conclusions of an earlier period. While there is always the liability, in any new, real, or supposed revelation of science, of the theological shout of warning or of contradiction, there is no less certain, and usually first, in point of time, the infidel scientific shout, that in this new discovery theology and religion are hopelessly exploded. Of course there are many theologians, and many physical and other scientists, who keep clear of everything of this character; who know enough of their own and other departments of knowledge to be above such course. But here it is that most of them originate. Some forty or fifty years ago leading chemical explorers attempted to abolish the word and the idea of vitality. Now, its existence is not only admitted, but the effort and anticipation is to evolve it out of inorganic matter. So, again, and more recently, biologists found species and variations so fixed and limited in their capacity of transition, that the variations of the human race, as to origin, were found impossible in any one of them. And, still more recently, this capacity of variation has become so expanded that it includes, not only all the varieties of the human race, but many, if not all, of the lower orders of creation. Theologians, in the mean time, adhered to the idea of life as a reality; to the origin of the race, in the divinely created man; to the creation of that man, in the Divine image of rationality, and moral and spiritual being. How far are these assertions of theology adjustable to those affirmed by science is the future problem, alike of the theological as of the physical and biological scientist. Such adjustment can only be anticipated, as the rightful claims of both are fully acknowledged and accepted.

A living writer in one of our popular science monthlies has endeavored to show the opposition of theologians to the progress of science. When he gets through, as he does not seem to have quite finished, he will find quite as abundant material, used in the same way, to demonstrate the opposition of scientists to such progress. The average scientist, as the average theologian, is familiar with the science imbibed in his youth, or boyhood, as infallible and unchangeable; and each alike, on the scientific grounds thus accepted, opposes the scientific novelty. There is scarcely an instance of any great scientific discovery which would not afford an illustration.

And here, it may be asked, is there not also a philosophy of religion and of theology, as of everything else? There is, of course; but it is very different from their science. Science, as we have seen, has to do with phenomena, facts, laws, unifying principles; or, as the schoolmen would have said, with "quiddities," the *quid*, the *quod*, and the *quomodo*. Philosophy has to do with them in the *quo*, with the *cur* and *quære*. Philosophy has been called the science of first principles. If by this be meant the principles to be assumed, in all science and scientific investigation, it may be admitted. But, evidently, we have gotten away from the ordinary conception of a science. The philosophy of a thing is its rationale, its immediate or ultimate cause. If, therefore, a science, it is the science of causes; that in which the phenomena and their laws alike find explanation. This ultimate Cause is the Divine Source and Origin of things; its first principles, what may be called secondary causes. With these, supposed or real, science begins. In view of them, it ventures or reaches certain conclusions; in some cases correctly, in others incorrectly.

We may, therefore, briefly sum up the result of our discussion by saying that theology is occupied with and exhibits the material of truth about God, and His relations to the world and to men, certified, systematized, unified; that religion is the knowing, feeling, and doing, as the effect of these truths, subjectively appropriated; and more or less wrought into the life. The philosophy of these is the divinely given religious nature, as related to its Divine Author, to the divinely given provision in Him, for that nature—to its full development and expansion of capacity, as of blessedness.

Professor Cooke's "Credentials of Science the Warrant of Faith."

Dawson's "Origin of the World According to Revelation and Science."

Kinnis's "Harmony of Bible with Science;" Reusch's "Nature and the Bible."

Harris's "Philosophical Basis of Theism."

Duke of Argyle's "Unity of Nature" and "Reign of Law."

Calderwood's "Relations of Science and Religion."

"Christianity and Science," Professor Peabody.

CHAPTER II.

SOURCES OF THEOLOGICAL TRUTH.

The two extremes of upon this subject of the naturalist and the purely supernaturalist, and the contrasted teaching of Scripture.—Relations of natural theology and revelation.—Revelation rests upon specific evidence.—Place here of natural presuppositions.—How revelation related to natural capacity.

THEOLOGY implies a known God. How is He known? In what manner has He actually made Himself known? How does He still bring Himself to human knowledge? Two extreme answers to this question have been given. One finds such knowledge given in the manifestations of nature and as entirely confined to these. The other finds it in special revelation; and all religious truth, in human conviction, of course, in many cases, with perversions and distortions, coming through primæval revelation. The first is that of deistic naturalism, with its *a priori* postulate of the impossibility of the miraculous or supernatural. The second is the extreme of the devout believer, jealous of any authority, or of any claim of Divine truth, in anything except the divinely revealed word. The first implies the absurdity that He who created man capable of communicating and of receiving communications by spoken and written words, is Himself wanting in the capacity which He conferred upon His creatures. The second, that He who created and fills the world with His wisdom, and goodness, and power, is nowhere, in that world, to be found.

In each of these extremes is a truth, if not distorted, at least one-sided. Taking the dictate of Scripture, we find both of these, as sources of truth about God, clearly recognized. Scripture, in its very existence and nature, involves the claim that God, "in different manners and different degrees," makes Himself known, through His selected human agents, in His authoritatively spoken and written word. No less does Scripture affirm and imply that He who thus extraordinarily reveals Himself does it, also, ordinarily, in His works—in the orderly arrangement of natural phenomena and their operations, the cosmos external; in the inner phenomena of human consciousness, knowing, feeling, willing, self-approving, and self-condemning, the inner cosmos of rational and moral experience. The nineteenth Psalm, for instance, implies and affirms both of these sources. The first six verses tell of the manifestations of God in the external world. The remaining eight tell of the revelation of His law. Law, *torah*, here, is the equivalent not only of revealed statute, but of revealed doing and character. So, in the first chapter of the Epistle to the Romans, the manifestation of God, in His created works, and the human obligation arising therefrom, is clearly asserted. In the second chapter of this same epistle, the obedience of the heathen to the law in their heart implies the same fact, the capacity of knowing this law, as also its Divine Author. The "unknown God" at Athens (Acts 17 : 22-31), it is implied, is known enough to be worshipped. Further, that in His real character, He ought to have been better known and differently worshipped. So too with the remonstrance of Paul and Barnabas to the Lycaonians (Acts 14 : 17). In these last cases, knowledge, capacity of knowledge, and accountability for its exercise are clearly implied. At the same time, knowledge additional is spoken of as imparted.

The *first* of these gives us natural theology, the *second* that of Scripture. The first related to the second, as part to the whole; as also illustrative and confirmative. Revelation includes natural theology plus its own peculiar material. This fact of revelation rests upon specific evidence. A *priori* presumptions may *anticipate*, but *cannot* prove it. At the same time, these presumptions have their value. They anticipate difficulties, and predispose to a certain conclusion. Some of these may be briefly considered.

First of all, specific revelation seems to be a necessity to the majority of the race; as reaching, in its intelligibility, all classes, all orders of mind and capacity. Supposing a perfect theology, in the philosophy of Plato; to how many could it be imparted? Revelation is the *via brevissima* of Divine wisdom, in its communications, to human ignorance and incapacity. It is for all. And it is in a form and manner to reach all.

Further, it meets another necessity of human nature, in the fact of its authoritative character. This is a want of the cultivated and philosophical, as well as the weak and ignorant. Has God spoken ? The distinct affirmative to this is as much needed by Newton or Kepler as by the humblest peasant or the little child.

Still further, such necessity may be seen, in the material of revelation, as supplementary to that of nature. Natural theology raises questions and encounters problems that it cannot solve. It cannot help asking, but cannot answer. "You may even give over," says one heathen philosopher, "all hopes of amending men's manners for the future, unless God be pleased to send some other person to instruct us." "Which of these opinions is true, some God must tell us," is the language of another. The material of revelation proves its necessity.

Last of all, revelation, in the light of experience, seems a necessity to the highest and purest form of civilization. Revealed religion rules and blesses the world; its power and influences point to its Divine origin.

Revelation as Related to Human Capacity.—Connected with this topic, the sources of material of Divine truth, are two others, as specially related to such truth contained in Scripture. One of these is the question of interpretation; the other is that of the relation of reason, or human capacity, to the substance of Divine revelation. As to the first, it may be said that whatever diversities, in the past, as to allegorical, mystical, symbolical, or spiritual interpretation, it is now an almost universally admitted principle that, as the revelations of law, of duty, of the Divine dealings and character, are given in human language, and in the forms of expression prevalent among their recipients, so, by the ordinary laws of language, their meaning must be ascertained. All other things being equal, the student who is best able to reproduce the conditions, objective and subjective, of those to whom the revelations were given, will be most successful in getting their meaning. If the language and its connection indicate literality, it must, then, be literally interpreted; if figurative, symbolical, or allegorical, then by the principles of each respectively. An undevout scholar, indeed, may in such case, and carrying out these principles, fail in getting the life and heart of that with which he is dealing; as may one of an opposite character, although comparatively ignorant, fully appreciate them. This, however, does not affect the general principle. The desideratum is both of these qualifications: the scholarship pervaded and quickened by a spirit of genuine earnestness and devotion.

The more difficult and contested question is the relation of reason, or human capacity, to these truths, when clearly and manifestly revealed. The word reason, it is here to be noted, in ordinary usage, flits often without any recognition of the fact, either by speaker or hearer, from one to the other of four distinct significations. Sometimes, for instance, it means the rationally intuitive power of cognizing necessary truth, the νους; sometimes the argumentative capacity, the analytic and synthetic power, the λογισμος; sometimes the capacity of appreciating or understanding, the διανοια; and, then, including all these, it means the whole mental capacity. The two main points of issue are, first, the power of reason or human capacity to receive truths incomprehensible; secondly, the capacity of reason or the necessary intuitive power, to receive what is really contradictory to its principles. To state the first clearly and distinctly is to answer it. Human capacity, or reason, in this sense, is constantly in the actual reception and usage of natural truths that are incomprehensible. *Omnia exeunt in mysterium.* Human language and expressions are full of incomprehensibles, from the infinitudes of space and duration to the infinitesimals of the atom and the molecule. If so in nature, then also in revelation. The distinction of apprehending and comprehending properly comes in here. We apprehend and discriminate, and find relations among things, in certain respects incomprehensible. If such incomprehensible fact come to us in revelation, we must accept it as we do with those that come to us in nature.

The second of these questions has given more difficulty—the relation of intuitive reason, not to incomprehensibles, but to contradictions, truths, or asserted truths in conflict with the principles of the rational nature, the intellectual or moral rational. In a genuine revelation and a really enlightened reason, such conflict is, of course, impossible. A contradictory is self-destructive. The assertion of a whole greater than the sum of its parts; of a circular triangle; of crossing parallel lines; of a malignant benevolence; or of filthy purity, are all of this class. Reason not only cannot construe, it cannot receive them as objects of contemplation, must reject them. If anything apparently of this character were found in a professed revelation, it would have to be rejected either as vitiating the whole, or as a human interpolation, or as misunderstood. The unbelieving effort has been to bring some of the material of the Old Testament, especially of its legislation, under this category. Some cases, doubtless, of these are difficulties and incomprehensibilities; and the effort must be to find out their explanation; to avoid the issue of rational and moral contradiction.

To sum up this point, we may say the relation of reason, of human capacity to revelation, is to ascertain and verify the fact of such revelation; to find out its meaning; the different ways in which that meaning is exhibited. When such meaning brings to view hitherto undiscernible truths, they must be reverently accepted upon the authority of their Divine Author. His revelations cannot be subjected to natural and finite limitations. In cases of apparent conflict with rational principles, intellectual or moral, as both of these proceed from Him, that conflict is only apparent. Patient and reverential investigation, and suspense as to hasty judgment, will, in due time, remove the apparent difficulty.

Robson's "The Bible ; its Revelation, Inspiration, and Evidence."
Briggs's "The Bible, the Church, and Reason."
Andrew's "God's Revelation of Himself to Man."
Bruce's "Chief End of Revelation."
Ollsen's "Revelation, Universal and Special."

CHAPTER III.

CANON OF SCRIPTURE: THAT OF OLD TESTAMENT.

Meaning of the word.—Collection of sacred books recognized by Christ and His Apostles.—Language of Josephus, of Philo, Son of Sirach, and the Talmud.—How Canon probably formed.—Allusions to it in early Christian writers.

The acceptance of the idea of a record of revelation immediately raises the question, What is this record; what its bounds and limitations? Revelation might be oral, and only for the individual and his contemporaries. It might involve a divinely inspiring influence upon the recipient, and yet be only for immediate and present purposes. Again, it might be for all time and for all men; revealed to inspired men, and placed in permanent, written form, for all coming generations. By this last we describe the canon of Scripture, the list of divinely revealed books, given through inspired men.

This word canon, it is to be borne in mind, has other significations. It meant, in earlier usage, the canon or list of articles of faith to be accepted—in other words, a creed. So, too, it was used to designate the list of books, inspired and uninspired alike, to be read in the churches. Again, and in more modern usage, it almost exclusively means the list of the inspired books of Scripture. In the second of these, the canon of the Church of England includes some of the apocryphal books. In the third sense, the canon of this Church is that of the divinely inspired books of the Old and New Testaments. For our purpose, we put aside all other meanings, and confine ourselves to the last, the inspired, authoritative books of Holy Scripture. How does it appear that such a collection was made? On what grounds is it now accepted? We naturally begin with the canon of the Old Testament.

Taking New Testament times as our point of departure, we find clear indication of the existence of such collection in the language of our Lord and that of the apostles. "Scripture," "the Scriptures," "the law," "the law and the prophets," "the law, the prophets, and the Psalms," are some of its modes of designation. With these, at times, is mention of particular writers—Moses, David, Isaiah—as familiar alike to speaker and hearers, and as of supreme Divine authority.

Contemporaneous with these New Testament writers and speakers are two Jewish writers, using similar language, and from whom a similar conclusion, as to these books, may be derived. Philo, born B.C. 20, wrote probably about A.D. 30 or 40°; Josephus, born 37 A.D., wrote about 85 or 90. Philo, thus about twenty years of age at the birth of our Lord, was about fifty at the time of the crucifixion; Josephus, born about the time of the conversion of St. Paul, and dying about the same time as St. John, as Jewish contemporaries of the Jewish speakers and writers of the

CANON OF SCRIPTURE: THAT OF OLD TESTAMENT. 21

New Testament, could only mean the same collection of authoritative Jewish Scriptures. The contemporaneousness of the two classes of speakers and writers excludes the possibility of change or of different material. Philo speaks of it, as does our Lord, in its threefold division—of "laws, oracles uttered by prophets, hymns and other books." Josephus speaks of it as the "five books of Moses, thirteen prophetical books, four of hymns and directions of life." Agreeing with this in substance is the threefold division of the son of Sirach, about 250 B.C., of "the law, the prophets, and the remaining books." Accordant with this is the language of the Talmud—beginning, as to its material, soon after the time of Ezra—as to "the law, the prophets, and the writings;" and the fact of their translation into the Septuagint about 200 B.C.

Taking, therefore, the time of our Lord, we find this threefold division in His language as in that of His Jewish contemporaries; this, in substance, agreeing with that of the Talmud, the son of Sirach, and the Septuagint. The different Jewish schools of thought—the Palestinian, the Babylonian, and the Alexandrian—agreeing substantially upon this point, would be a check upon each other in any attempted change or variation. Two facts are thus made manifest: first, the existence of this collection; secondly, that its books held a peculiar position of pre-eminence. They were not, as many suppose, the whole of Jewish or Hebrew literature extant at this or any other period. There is evidence of other the apocryphal books, for instance; and of others earlier and later, not contained or recognized in the Hebrew canon.

Accordant with this is the testimony of Christian writers of the three or four centuries following. Justin Martyr, writing during the first half of the second century, mentions sixteen of the Old Testament writers in his controversy with the Jew Trypho. The Talmud, already alluded to as contemporaneous in its oral form with Sirach and the Septuagint, put in its written form during the first four centuries of Christianity, in this latter speaks of this same collection, and of the authorship of particular books. With slight variation the Old Testament canon, in the catalogue of Melito of Sardis, 179, corresponds with that of these Jewish writers. The same may be said of that of Origen, 220, of Athanasius, 325, of Cyril, Augustine, and Jerome, of the next two centuries. Later Jewish catalogues have the same threefold division of the law, the prophets, and the Hagiographa. In some cases they divide them differently in their parts, include smaller books differently in longer ones. The Apocrypha, never accepted by the Jews, was added by the Council of Trent. But it is not fully accepted even by the best scholarship of the Church of Rome.

How this canon was formed, and what the successive steps to its completion, it is difficult to determine. While there is no specific historical evidence sustaining the tradition of its formation by Ezra, yet the circumstances of his position and times, as his peculiar work, would naturally lead to something of this character.

The argument in such case is: any other man, of ordinary good sense, having Ezra's task, and with these materials at hand, would have pursued the course supposed. The same may be said as to Nehemiah. Certainly it must have been begun at this time, but most probably at an earlier date. The effort of Jewish scholarship, as of Jewish religious feeling, would be to co-operate in such undertaking. Evidence of such scholarship and of such religious interest is not wanting. The material of the Talmud and the Targums indicates usage of these books, and interest in them; imply familiarity with them, and reverence toward them. The hostile effort of Antiochus Epiphanes to destroy the sacred books of Judaism would by reaction, as with the Christians under Domitian, with books of the New Testament, lead to the opposite result of their fuller verification. As already intimated, they are all found translated in the Septuagint. The Hebrew canon, in the time of our Lord, is now that of modern Judaism.

The simplest explanation of these facts is, that these books, each one, as actually given, and at the time, in its known author, verified itself as a divinely given book, as was the case subsequently with those of the New Testament. Allusions are made to portions of them in Old Testament narrative. The five books of Moses, as found among the Samaritans, must have been collected, and in shape, not very long after the time of Ezra. Directions are given in Old Testament narrative, requiring other portions to be put in writing. "We know," says Professor Cave, "that Moses set an example of an authoritative canon in his five books of the law. There is good reason for saying that the schools of the prophets, following the Mosaic example, constituted themselves the guardians of the several prophetical writings, which they preserved, to form a steadily increasing whole, until the open vision of prophecy ceased." The work of Ezra, as of Jewish scholarship, like that of Christian, with the books of the New Testament, would be to separate them and keep them separate from all others. And the fact of the universal acceptance of this result affords presumption that it was done in a satisfactory manner. The hypothesis of this, as the work of a divinely inspired man or men of "canonic inspiration," to use the language of the writer just quoted, fully meets, and only fully meets all the facts, and the demands of the case. The accepted work of after scholarship is thus simply to ascertain what has been done; what are really these divinely given books to God's chosen people.

Questions as to particulars of any of these books, and their writers or sources, say of the portions of Genesis, the Pentateuch or Hexateuch, of the Deutero-Isaiah, of the Book of Daniel, or the Maccabean Psalms, these belong to other departments of investigation. However answered, the canon as it stands does so upon the later authentication of our Lord, as of earlier and later Jewish scholarship; as, also, upon the judgment of modern Judaism, and of the Christian Church accepting it.

Etheridge's "Introduction to Hebrew Literature."
Cave's "Inspiration of the Old Testament."
Simon's "Theocratic Literature."
Kirkpatrick's "Divine Library of the Old Testament."
Girdlestone's "Foundations of the Faith."
Rabbi Wise's "Pronaos of the Old Testament."
Paterson Smith's "Old Documents and the New Bible."
Buhl's "Canon and Text of the Old Testament."
Driver's "Introduction to the Old Testament.

CHAPTER IV.

CANON OF SCRIPTURE: THAT OF NEW TESTAMENT.

The two questions.—How to be answered.—Early traces of usage of the four Gospels.—Patristic testimony as to these and other books of New Testament.—That of heretical and heathen writers.—Early versions.—Indications of early, and wide circulation.

Two questions, tacitly implied in the preceding discussion, as to the canon of the Old Testament, have been more specifically raised in regard to that of the New Testament. First, What constitutes a canonical book? secondly, When was the canon, the list of them as a whole, completed? To the first has been the reply: The fact of inspired authorship, either apostles or contemporaneous disciples of prophetic endowment; these last known, accepted, and thus endorsed by the primitive Church. Out of the twenty-seven books of the New Testament, twenty-three are by apostles, and, therefore, included in the promise of the Master, as to the Paraclete, to give them all needed Divine aid, in the deliverance of their testimony. Paul, as called to the apostleship, of course as an apostle, came within the terms of this assurance; specifically claims to speak and write under Divine influence and with Divine authority.

Besides the apostles, however, we find mention of

other disciples endowed with prophetic gifts: Agabus, twice alluded to; Ananias, in connection with the conversion of Paul; as also allusions to similar gifts in one of the epistles to the Church at Corinth. The association of St. Luke with the Apostle Paul, and of Mark with Peter, of course gave them peculiar opportunities for the preparation of their books. But the unquestioning reception of those books from the beginning, the manner of that reception, as on a level with the others, and this by the whole Church, would indicate the recognition by contemporaries of their own divinely conferred qualifications for such undertaking. The same may be said of the Epistle to the Hebrews. If by St. Paul, of course apostolic and inspired; if by Apollos, then as one divinely fitted for his work; if by St. Luke, then either as shaping the material of St. Paul, or, as in his gospel, from his own divinely conferred endowment. The fact in regard to them all is this, their acceptance by those to whom they were given; the testimony, thus involved, as to known prophetic capacity. The testimony of subsequent witnesses, Christian, heretical, and heathen writers, is not simply to an opinion, but to a fact; not that they, as individuals, think these to be divinely authenticated, but that they have been thus accepted from the beginning. In answer to the first question, therefore, we say, the canon is thus the list of the writings of inspired men, as to the events and truths recorded in them.

The second of these questions, When was the canon,

as a whole, completed? is less easy to answer; and this, in view of the different centres of religious life and influence, the different churches to which these books were first given or sent. Each one of these constituted the evidential centre to its own special book. Its task was to communicate this book to other neighboring churches, and through these to reach the whole Church; receiving, in turn, from any of these, other books of the same character. To use the idea of Bentley, any such book was certified and authenticated, listed, canonized immediately, in its intelligent reception, by the church or community to which it was addressed. When the Epistle, for instance, to the Corinthians or to the Philippians was received by the hand of Paul's messenger, as St. Paul's writing or message, and thus recognized, then and there all questions as to its character and authority were settled. The work of such church, as we have said, was to let this be known to neighboring churches; as when these received a similar epistle to communicate to them in return. These communications seem to have been rapid. The presence of common opposition and danger, as the sympathy of a common faith and hope, and of everything connected with it, would thus hasten this process of mutual communication. Books of a different character, like the Gospels, not like the epistles, addressed to a particular community, but of interest to all, would, from their emanating centres, extend to the whole Christian community of the empire, and even beyond. As a matter of fact, and showing that this must have been the process, the latest certified books are those, not like the epistles sent to Churches, or the gospels for all the churches, but those to individuals, like the epistles of John or that to Philemon. The Council of Laodicea, 360, and that of Carthage, 397, found the canon completed and in full acceptance; they did not settle it. That result had already been providentially, divinely accomplished, and in a way that took it out of the hands of mere human agency and authority.

As having its special interest in this investigation, we first look at indications of the four Gospels. The first specific mention of them as a whole is by Irenæus of Lyons. He speaks of the number four, of the writers by name, and of the peculiarities of their material. Similar language, as to the number of these gospels, is used by Clement of Alexandria and by Tertullian of Carthage. This was during the last half of the second century, and, in one case, by a man who had conversed with contemporaries of the apostles.

Earlier than this, however, is the language of Justin Martyr, 90 A.D. to 166 A.D., as to "the memorials of the apostles" read in the churches. As Irenæus, born 140 A.D., was twenty-six years old at the time of Justin's martyrdom, the strong presumption is that these "memorials" are the Gospels. The interval is not sufficient for the disappearance of the one and the coming in of the other of a different character. The memory of Irenæus, it may be said, went back of the time of which Justin was writing. When, moreover, we find that Tatian, a disciple of Justin, prepared the Diatessaron, or harmony of these four Gospels, the presumption becomes a reasonable certainty. The Didache, earlier perhaps than any of these, uses materials from the Gospels, and seems to know of portions of them; of St. Matthew certainly, and perhaps of St. Luke. But it gives no list or names of books. It would thus appear that these Gospels, as four, were known in the first third of the second century; within thirty years of the death of the Apostle John.

As to the materials of the New Testament, as it was gathered into a collection, it would soon naturally be listed. The wonder here is, the early period in which they seem to have been made. One of the earliest is that of the Muriatorian canon. This, from allusions in it, seems to have been written about 140 A.D.— within a generation of the Apostle John, and twenty-eight years before the death of Polycarp. This contains all the books of the New Testament except Hebrews, James, Peter, and second and third epistles of John. It speaks of an Apocalypse of Peter doubtfully. Following is the catalogue of Origen, 185 to 220 A.D., which includes all of the present canon except James and Jude. These last he quotes in other parts of his works as of authority. This writer, in his extant works, quotes two thirds of the material of the New Testament, and the whole contents of the four Gospels. Had the New Testament been lost, "it might have been recovered," to use the language of Dr. Tregelles, "from these books of Origen." With

Eusebius is mention of all, with his well-known division of spurious, questioned, and accepted books; the two last included in the present canon. Jerome has the same list as the present. He speaks, doubtfully, of Hebrews; but elsewhere treats it as canonical.

Corroborative of such evidence is the fact of the existence and usage of the Syriac and old Latin versions. The former was probably made as early as the middle of the second century, and agrees with the present except second and third John, Jude, and Revelation. The Latin versions have disappeared, or, rather, were driven out of circulation by the Vulgate. The Diocletian persecution, in its specific effort to destroy the sacred books of the Christians, not only proved such lists to be in existence, but led to clearer discrimination and more decided effort on the part of Christians to preserve these books, and to keep them apart from all others; as does Eusebius' threefold classification show that they were not received without careful examination. The Apocalypse as identified with peculiar views of the millennium, in certain localities was for a time suspected and doubted; as were the smaller, and individual epistles, later in finding circulation and acceptance.

The evidence thus afforded, in specific lists of these books, by different writers, thus covering the first four centuries of Christian history, has, in this form, its peculiar value. But this value is greatly increased when we bear in mind the manner in which the authors of these lists estimated and used the books thus spoken of, and what was the estimate and use by their contemporaries. These lists, say, of Origen, of Athanasius, of Jerome, are the skeleton. The material of these books, thus listed, as used by these writers, is to be found upon every page of their writings, and filling volumes; found, also, in all the Christian literature of their times; this, so to speak, gives the skeleton, flesh, and blood, and bones, and skin, and makes it a living and speaking organism. Origen, for instance, gives us a list of these books, accepted by the Church, as authoritative Divine teaching. But Origen, as we have seen, quotes two thirds of the contents of the books in his extant writings; and in this, the whole contents of the four Gospels; as in his Hexapla he reveals his familiarity with the contents of the Old Testament. "There are," says Lardner, "perhaps more and longer quotations of the small volume of the New Testament in the writings of Tertullian than of all the works of Cicero, though of so uncommon excellence for thought and style, in the writing of all characters for several ages." So, too, as illustrative of the circulation of books among the Christian communities, Professor Norton calls attention to the fact that two hundred copies of Tatian's Diatessaron, compiled from the Gospels, was found by Theodoret among the membership of a single church, and that their place was easily supplied by copies of the Gospels; Tatian himself having adopted gnostic views in his writings, and being considered as heretical. This pervasion of Christian literature, with the material of the New Testament, practical and controversial, and the position of authority which it holds, gives a significance to these lists, which immeasurably increases their importance.

It is to be further borne in mind that the opportunities and means of reproducing these books of the New Testament, at the time of which we are speaking, were much more abundant than during some of the centuries following. It is a very common mistake to identify the costliness and consequent scarcity of books, say, in the tenth or twelfth centuries, with the conditions of the second and the third. They were very different. The cheapness of slave labor, as copyists, and the abundance of material for production, made it easy to make books in large numbers and at cheap rate. Andrews Norton, in his "Genuineness of the Gospels," gives particulars, in regard to this point, not only showing the cheapness of production, but the actual numbers of certain books at one time in circulation. His estimate is that, at the close of the second century, with a Christian population of at least three millions, there must have been sixty thousand copies of the New Testament, or one for every fifty, in circulation. These facts, as bearing upon the general subject of the reliability of the evidence as to the canon, are full of significance.

   Tregelles, on " Printed Text of the New Testament."
   Andrews Norton, on " The Genuineness of the Gospels."
   Salmon's " Introduction to Books of the New Testament."
   Charteris, on " New Testament Scriptures."
   Harman's " Introduction to the Holy Scriptures."
   Westcott on " Canon of the New Testament."

CHAPTER V.

INSPIRATION OF SCRIPTURE.

Inspiration naturally possible.—Question for believers.—New Testament evidence of it.—Language of the Master as to His own inspiration; as to that of His Apostles and chosen witnesses; as that of Old Testament.—Claims of the Apostles, themselves, as those of Old Testament writers.—Forms in which they are made.—Difficulties urged, and reply.—What really implied in inspiration.

The fact that there is a canon, or listed collection of books, from which all others are excluded, immediately suggests the inquiry as to the basis of such collection. What is there common in these books, and bringing them together? what is there unique and peculiar, separating them from all others? We are thus led to that which is their peculiar and differentiating element—their inspiration. The truths of these books may sometimes be found in other books, and wherever thus found are Divine; whether in Christian books, as those of Baxter or Leighton, or in books outside of Christian literature. But the books themselves and their writers do not come under the term inspired. Books are Divine or inspired as the writings of men divinely fitted for giving them to the world. Strictly, only persons are inspired; the books are so called as coming from such persons.

The two preliminary questions here are the possibility and the fact of inspiration. The first, the possibility, presents no difficulty. It is as to the Divine capacity of action. Is there Divine capacity of communication, whether in the use of natural, ordinary agencies, or of those that are extraordinary, with that which is human? Who can answer this question in the negative? Can it be thought a thing incredible that God, the Creator of man's capacities, should be able to communicate truth to him in this way? The question answers itself. If man needs it, God can and may be expected to do it.

In the line, moreover, of such anticipation, as rational, may be noted the beliefs and opinions on this subject, not only of Jews and Christians, but of those outside of the circle of the Old and New Testament revelation. Whether all such ideas and claims of inspiration, outside of this circle, were unfounded and false, cannot and need not be asserted. We can only say, that if any of them were genuine and accomplished their divinely intended purpose, the evidence, as is that of the Old and New Testament, has not been preserved. The fact of prevalent ideas and beliefs has, however, its significance. The unbelieving inference has been, all these were counterfeits; so, therefore, those of Judaism and Christianity. The believing inference is just the opposite. It is not certain that all these were counterfeits. But, if so, counterfeits always imply a genuine, somewhere or somehow. That men should, in so many forms, anticipate and naturally believe in this fact, implies the correlation of this fact not only to the convictions, but to the moral and spiritual necessities of human nature.

This matter, however, is one more particularly for Christian believers, those who accept the evidence, historical, moral, and otherwise, of the truth and genuineness of the Christian record. The apostles, for instance, were first heard by the unbelieving Jews and Gentiles as uninspired men; uninspired witnesses of certain events and transactions coming under their cognizance. After the conversion of these unbelievers they listened to the same apostles, as inspired witnesses, of these same facts, as also to their real meaning. It is a waste of time to argue the question or urge the authority of inspiration with a man who questions the historic credibility of the New Testament. Prior to inspiration is this previous question of the genuineness, authenticity, and credibility of the books claimed to be inspired.

So again, the distinction, more emphasized in late discussions, and helping to remove some of the difficulties of the subject, of revelation from inspiration, needs to be kept in mind. In many cases they went together; but in others they were separated, and in all need to be distinguished. There was, for instance, revelation to the whole camp of Israel at Sinai, of the majesty and will of Jehovah. There was inspiration to Moses to write the ten words and what followed for permanent remembrance. So, too, many of the earlier manifestations to patriarchs, as also of a later period, may not have included the inspiring influence. There were revelations to Balaam; and, at one supreme moment, there was an inspiration, driving him against his wish to proclaim the success of Israel. Our effort now is to find out as to this latter inspiration.

Deferring anything like a definition, until we have examined the phenomena, we begin with the New Testament. Our point of departure, as our ultimate authority, is the person and teaching of our blessed Lord. This teaching has reference to three spheres of inspiration: first, that of His own teaching; secondly, that of His apostles and accredited witnesses; third, that of Old Testament writers. We begin with the first: His claim to speak with Divine authority.

"As the Father gave Me charge, so I speak." "The words that I speak unto you, they are spirit and they are life." "He that sent Me is true; and I speak to the world those things which I have heard of Him." "As the Father hath taught Me, so I speak." "Whosoever followeth Me shall not abide in darkness, but have the light of life." "Even as the Father said unto Me, so I speak." There can be no doubt as to the meaning of these and similar declarations.

And as our Lord thus affirms the Divine authority of His own declarations, so does He give assurance of a Divine influence which would impart like authority to those of His apostles. Their work was to testify of Him. In that testimony, of course, there would be constant recurrence to acts and words of His, coming under their own observation, and in their own hearing.

Natural memory would be used in the report; but there would be also a Divine influence, aiding that memory, recalling all things as they had taken place. So, too, as to other things; their understanding of His character and work. But with this, also, a Divine influence, "taking these things of Him," and revealing them in their full significance. As witnesses of Him, in this work of their apostleship—not in other matters or undertakings—but in this, their appointed work, the Paraclete, the Spirit of wisdom and of knowledge, would be with them, and in them, and give truth and authority to all their teachings and declarations.

Among these assurances, the first in point of time was in connection with the sending forth of the twelve (Matt. 10 : 19, 20). "It is not ye that speak," is His language in contemplation of a certain exigency, "but the Spirit of your Father, that speaketh in you." Again in Luke 12 : 11, in telling them of dangers to be encountered in His service, the same assurance is given: "Take no thought, be not anxious," as to the manner or the matter, $\pi\omega\varsigma$ η $\tau\iota$, "how or what ye shall speak." "The Holy Ghost shall teach you in the same hour what ye ought to speak." So, again, later in His prediction of the destruction of Jerusalem, and of difficulties and persecutions connected with their work in preaching the Gospel (Mark 13 : 11 ; Luke 21 : 14), the same assurance is given, with the additional promise, "I will give you a mouth, and wisdom which all your adversaries shall not be able to gainsay nor to resist."

Throwing light upon all these, and expanding their meaning, is His declaration at the last supper, of the Paraclete going with them, and recalling all things to their remembrance, revealing His person and work, leading them into the whole truth, and showing them things to come. All these, closing in the promise given just before the ascension (Acts 1 : 1-8), when they are reminded of "the promise of the Father," already given, and receive their last assurance of the power of the Holy Ghost, as they witnessed for Him " in Jerusalem, and in Samaria, and to the ends of the earth." Manifestly there is, in these declarations, the authoritative word of the Master to the affirmed inspiration of these, His chosen witnesses. And, as with these, as we saw in the discussion on the canon, so with others called to their special work—to Paul, to Barnabas, admitted to the apostolate ; to Agabus or Apollos ; to Luke or Mark, receiving the prophetic gift, speaking under the power of the same Divine Spirit and with the same Divine authority.

And as our Lord thus gave assurance of this inspiration to the apostles, so these apostles themselves distinctly claim it. "The word of God, which ye have heard of us" (1 Thess. 11 : 13), is one of these declarations. "What I write unto you are the commandments of the Lord" (1 Cor. 14 : 37) is another. "I received the Gospel by revelation of Jesus Christ ; not from man, nor by man, but through Jesus Christ from God" (Gal. 1 : 12). "We are of God. He that heareth God, heareth us" (1 John 4 : 6). So, too, as to forms and modes of expression, in which it is implied. "It seemed good to the Holy Ghost and to us" (Acts 15:28). "The Spirit speaketh expressly" (1 Tim. 4:1). "We speak in the words which the Holy Ghost teacheth" (1 Cor. 2:4, 7, 10, 12, 13). "We have the Spirit" (Eph. 3:5). "I was in the Spirit" (Rev. 1:10; 4:2). Evidently the claim is here asserted of the actual possession, of the power promised to them by the Master.

But question has here arisen as to the adjustment of these assurances and claims with certain recorded facts of apostolic experience. One of these is the conference of the fifteenth chapter, in the Acts of the Apostles, and the conclusion as the result of that conference. Another is the inability of Peter fully to see the meaning of his vision until after his conversation with Cornelius. Another is the contention of Paul and Barnabas as to the propriety of giving Mark a second trial. And the last is the inability of Peter to see his inconsistency of action until his attention was called to it by the rebuke of Paul.

To these difficulties the general reply may be made: inspiration is not omniscience. It is insight given with reference to a particular object, and in a variety of ways. Still further, if these cases constituted inconsistency, the disciples and the writer of the book do not seem to recognize it. The process by which an inspired man was brought to a conclusion, of which he could be divinely assured, was, in different cases, a very different one. Peter needed to be led and instructed in a peculiar manner before he could clearly see the fact of the full extension of the Gospel to the Gentiles. He needed, again, by the rebuke of Paul, to see that he was acting inconsistently with this truth, which he had previously reached in the house of Cornelius. The same Divine process of imparting light to an inspired conclusion was afforded in the discussions of the Apostolic Council. The contention of Paul and Barnabas was not as to their teaching, but as to the merits of an individual. Most readers think Paul was right; but Mark's subsequent experience seems to justify the view of Barnabas. But whichever was right, it was not a matter of inspiration.

So far, then, as regards the inspiration of the Master Himself, and that of the apostles in this, His own language, and in theirs reaffirming, we find it clearly and emphatically asserted. As applicable to their teaching orally given, it is equally so to that teaching in written form. As the wisdom of man has made manifest that this is the best form in which to place truth and corrrectly perpetuate it, the wisdom of God would not select one that is inferior.

We are thus led to the kindred question of the inspiration of the Old Testament. Here we have not only the affirmations of the Master and of the apostles, but of the Old Testament writers themselves. We begin with the first. Prior to specific examination of this there are two general presumptions to be noted as of special significance. One of these is the ordinary course of our Lord, and of the apostles, as to Judaism and Jewish Scriptures. While their real work was to subvert Judaism, especially in its rabbinic form, their language and course upheld and honored the Jewish Scriptures; they even affirm that in these Scriptures is a Divine sanction to their work. No less important, as in the same line of inference, is the usage and peculiar idea of the word prophet—not merely a predicter, but one speaking under Divine enlightenment and direction; organs of Divine communication, under Divine guidance, and proclaiming, "Thus saith Jehovah." This term, used both in the Old and New Testaments, carries with it this implication. Taking with us these presumptions, we look at some of the declarations of these different witnesses in regard to this subject.

We begin with those of our Lord. "David spake by the Holy Ghost." "God's word cannot be broken." "The Scriptures testify of Me." "The Scriptures must be fulfilled." "All things must be fulfilled which were written in the law of Moses, and in the prophets, and in the Psalms concerning Me." "Beginning at Moses and all the prophets, He expounded unto them, in all the Scriptures, the things concerning Himself." These are a few out of many; but they are sufficient. It is to be said that in His appeals to Old Testament Scripture it was as ultimate, as Divine in its authority.*

---

* The point has been recently made, especially in connection with the declarations of our Lord in regard to particulars of the Old Testament, as to whether such declaration is, in all cases, to be regarded as final.

The same is to be said as to the apostles. Their preaching was to show, from the Old Testament, as divinely predicting, that Jesus was the Messiah, and

The doubt in this case is urged upon two grounds: First, upon that of the limitations of our Lord's knowledge, in the very fact of His humanity. Secondly, supposing His knowledge perfect, as extending to His actual declarations, His object was, not to settle questions of criticism and history, but to reveal Himself and His work; in so doing to employ the terms then in use, and adapt Himself to the intelligence of His hearers. We examine the first.

Jesus Himself, it is urged, speaks of things which He did not know: "increased in wisdom and stature;" was "surprised" at things as they sometimes took place. If limited, it is asked, in the conditions of His humanity in these respects, why not in others? Why not as to the authorship and time of the composition of a Psalm, or as to that of certain portions of the Pentateuch? Why not regard Him in this, His human knowledge, as in common with that of His age and time? To this the reply is direct and decisive. While our Lord knew the limitations within which He was not to speak, He knew also His knowledge as to those things of which He ought and did speak. It would almost seem as if some of His declarations were anticipative of such question. "What we know we speak; what we have seen we testify." "I speak as My Father hath taught Me." "What I should say and what I should speak the Father gave Me commandment." "As I hear, I judge; and the word that ye hear is not Mine, but the Father's, which sent Me." In the light of these declarations, it may be said that He knew His own human limitations; and knowingly, from the Spirit which dwelt in Him without measure, spoke and taught authoritatively within those limitations. The highest form of mere uninspired knowledge is this, which includes its own limitations and keeps its utterances within them. Was that of Him, who, perfect humanity in union with Deity, and even in that humanity filled with the Holy Ghost, the Spirit of knowledge and wisdom, less? What He positively said He knew; and He always thus unhesitatingly spoke, as knowing that He knew.

But, then, as to the second, it is further asked, supposing this perfect that this Messiah was the predicted head, not of an earthly, but of a heavenly and spiritual kingdom. From Peter's first sermon to his Jewish countrymen, knowledge in Himself, as to all His affirmations, did He in such affirmation endorse, or intend to endorse, all the meanings of the terms employed, and in the sense in which He knew Himself to be understood? This is a different question, and demands careful consideration. Words, it is to be recognized, have an etymological, and they may have a later contemporaneous and popular meaning. No one who now speaks of a man as a lunatic means to say that the moon made him so. So, again, to say that a man is a villain, does not hold us to the assertion that he lives, or ever lived, in a village. We speak of the sun rising and setting without becoming responsible for the Ptolemaic theory. So in numberless other cases. The speaker, in any such case, is held to the sense in which he knows that he is understood. Our blessed Lord and the inspired writers, to be intelligible, must employ the terms and forms of expression in usage among their hearers. The same thing may be said as to historical allusion, or to known characters even in well-known works of fiction. Supposing the Book of Jonah, or that of Ruth, to have been a fiction, and accepted as such by hearers and speakers; illustrations from them, in our Lord's teaching, might have been anticipated.

But supposing any such fiction, known as such by a speaker, but regarded by his hearer as a genuine history, be used by that speaker in argument or teaching, as historical truth, and thus to the establishing of his conclusions. This would not be *argumentum ad hominem*, as it is sometimes represented, but *argumentum ad ignorantiam*—taking advantage of ignorance to reach a conclusion which the material did not really sustain. A speaker, under the law of contract, is held to the sense in which he knows himself to be understood by his hearer. He is so morally as well as legally. The significance of this principle must be recognized, as we look at these, our Lord's declarations. Much more, too, when, upon this accepted sense, depends the validity of His conclusion. Those Old Testament books were regarded as sacred truth; their sacredness associated with their authorship. Upon this basis the to Paul's last appeal to them at Rome, this was the invariable course pursued. No effort or specific affirmation is made as to the Divine source or authority of the Old Testament. It was always assumed and implied, on one side, always accepted as beyond doubt by the other. Such specific affirmations are afterward made in later Christian instruction. But, with Jewish hearers, it was not needed, would have been a gratuitous impertinence.

Among these latter are those of 2 Tim. 3 : 15, 16 ; 1 Pet. 1 : 10, 11, 12 ; 2 Pet. 1 : 19, 20, 21. The different readings of the first, "all Scripture is inspired," and "every inspired Scripture," does not affect the issue as to the Divine origin of the Old Testament; and the two others affirm its prophetic character and fulfilment in the events of the New Testament.

conclusion rests. When He said, "Moses wrote of Me," and "David said" thus and so of Me, in certain Old Testament books, He was speaking to those who accepted such origin and authorship. In that acceptation His argument found its conclusiveness. Suppose, for instance, He had said, "Some unknown writer or redactor of the time of Josiah, in a book which you think was written by Moses, wrote of Me." What would have been the reply ? Or, again, some unknown psalmist of the Maccabean times said in a psalm which you think was written by David, "the Lord said" thus and so of Me. Supposing these hearers to have kept themselves from stoning Him on the spot, what would have been the natural reply to such an argument ? Would it not have been, "What do we care for unknown writers of the Josian or the Maccabean age ? If Moses wrote and David spoke, as we believe they did, we are ready to hear them." Manifestly the common postulate with speaker and hearer, in an argument, is needed to give such argument its validity. Popular apprehensions cannot be used to establish truths, unless themselves truthful.

But how as to these Old Testament writers themselves? Do they claim to speak under Divine guidance and influence? The reply is best given in their own language.

"Jehovah said to me, Go and speak to this people" (Isa. 6 : 9). "Thus saith Jehovah" (Isa. 43 : 1). "The hand of Jehovah was upon me." "The word of Jehovah came to me." "The heavens were opened, and I saw visions of God" (Ezek. 1 : 1–3). "The word of the Lord came unto me, saying" (Ezek. 6 : 1). So also Jer. 23 : 9 ; 2 : 12 ; 7 : 23 ; Amos 3 : 1 ; 7 : 1 ; 9 : 1–3. These are but a few out of many. As in the language of our Lord, and that of the apostles, there can be no difficulty or doubt as to the fact meant to be asserted—that of Divine influence and guidance. These declarations, taken in connection with those of the New Testament, show, further, this influence and guidance as not only extending to prediction and to moral precept, but to other portions of Old Testament material. They are all spoken of alike in the New Testament. John 10 : 35, "Scripture cannot be broken." Facts and doctrines are treated as inseparable ; the precept or doctrine is in the fact, in ritual as in moral action, Heb. 9 : 18, "The Holy Ghost signifying," through these, certain Divine realities. So, too, with actions and sentiments of good men, of an improper as of a proper character. We have the record of David's weakness and sin, of Solomon's idolatry, of Job's impatience, of the erroneous arguments of his friends, of the complaints of Jeremiah, of the weakness of Hezekiah. The record in all these particulars has its divinely intended uses—is for the instruction of all, of all coming generations.

Such, then, as to the fact of inspiration, both of the Old and of the New Testament. We approach, now, the more disputed point of its character; what it implies; what in it is essential; what some of its incidentals? Is there any one word under which its character can be described; which gives what may be called a theory of inspiration? It is a Divine, and yet a human result; under a Divne Agent, and yet in connection with human personality. Each of these factors, Divine and human, act; and in such manner that the integrity of each is unimpaired. Not only the human personality, but the peculiar individualities of this personality, as manifest in the contents of the inspired books, find their place. As one of these personalities—the Divine—is infinite, and is thus, to some degree, incomprehensible in His operations, so any theory of these operations must be imperfect. We may examine some of the forms in which it has been affirmed.

One of these is what has been called the mechanical —that which eliminates the human personality, and makes the inspired man a mere machine in the hand of the Omnipotent Inspirer. Whether ever consistently held, it has now few, if any, advocates. Its main importance just now is, that those who attempt the opposite extreme—that of eliminating, not the human, but the Divine Agent, in the fact of inspiration, and to make it out purely a natural one—usually begin by representing their opponents, and of whatever class, as holding this, the "old traditional view" and explanation. It is sufficient to have described it.

This last, the natural, and as the greatest extreme from the mechanical, may briefly be described. This is inspiration of the whole man, in his highest physical, mental, and moral condition, as he is brought in contact with great truths and sentiments, comes under their power, and gives to them expression—that of the orator or poet in his best moments of natural inspiration. This, the rational and moral elevation of the human agent, was that of the Hebrew prophet, of the Christian apostle. If it be urged that this is spoken of as Divine, the reply is, "All that man has is divinely given, his natural powers, as his outward surroundings." As the inspiration, through the elevation of these natural powers, exercised and quickened under these divinely arranged outward conditions, it is properly described as Divine. It is thus a Divine gift, and power for all time, to be anticipated in every age of the world. In other words, it is naturally supernatural, if this last word ought ever to be used.

But to this there are two fatal difficulties. It does not correspond with the facts; and it really gets rid of what it attempts to explain. An inspiration, without an extraordinary Divine influence upon the inspired man, is in conflict with the whole tenor of Scripture teaching, already quoted. This fact of Bible inspiration cannot be brought within the category of mere natural agencies; and this explanation does violence to the terms in which it is described. The inspired man may have been, in the elevation of his highest and best rational and moral moments. The outward environment may have been of the most suggestive and favorable character. But there was something else, producing, it may be, this very elevation, and using these outward circumstances, distinct from, however, and above them—the personal Divine Spirit of Divine truth and wisdom.

Akin to this, and with like defect, to some degree, is that which has been called gracious inspiration. This, while recognizing the personal action of the Spirit of God upon the spirit of man, at the same time identifies it with the ordinary enlightening and sanctifying influence of the blessed Spirit upon the minds and hearts of believers. His agency to the revelation and certification of new truth, upon the specially selected prophet or apostle, is thus only the same as that of His enlightening and sanctifying agency in the spiritual life. The holiest man is the most fully inspired prophet, and all holy men are inspired.

These two things, doubtless, may, and, perhaps, ordinarily, did go together. They did so, perhaps, with Elijah and Paul; but how with Jonah or Balaam or Caiaphas? Ordinarily, it would seem that holy men were selected for such work. But not necessarily. A man of ordinary spiritual attainment might thus be selected, and another of higher spiritual character, but of inferior natural gifts, be left aside. The case of Jonah is almost as suggestive as that of Balaam or of Caiaphas. But whatever such capacity, natural, moral, or spiritual, there was something else. An inspired prophet is not, necessarily, although ordinarily, a man of the highest spiritual character and attainment. On the other hand, a holy man is not, thereby, an inspired prophet. The two things, if not always separated, must always be distinguished. This view, like the one preceding, gets rid of the idea of authoritative inspiration.

Somewhat different from either of these is what has been called partial inspiration; partial, sometimes as to the different books, sometimes as to the material of the same book; involving thus the idea of different degrees of inspiration. The law, it may be, and the prophets, with some; but not the historical books. With others, it is the material of prediction, and precept, and specific declaration, but not that, as in Paul's epistles, of reasoning; or, as in the Gospels, of narrative.

The element of truth, in this view, is that of the variety of the Divine operation, in its modes and manifestations. It is here, as it is in all Divine operations, manifoldness in unity. The unity, here, is the one authoritative, inspiring Divine Agent and agency. In this, its Divine identity, it baffles all finite qualification or quantification. The inspired writers themselves make no such effort. The Scriptures, as we have seen, in the language of our Lord, are spoken of as a whole, and are spoken of as alike authoritative.

Sometimes it is so under the word "Scripture;" sometimes where their threefold division is indicated. The idea of inspiration, moreover, as related to historical record, or to processes of reasoning, presents no rational difficulty. Men exercise upon each other similar influences, aiding their memory of facts, and their processes of reasoning, without any interference either with rational or moral personality. If so with the power of the spirit of man, much more so with the Spirit of God. The inspired writers are the only capable witnesses in this matter. Their testimony recognizes no such distinction; rather implies and affirms the contrary.

But, if thus extended to the whole of Scripture, in what sense? Is it to the words? And, if so, was it verbally dictated? These two ideas are distinct. We take the latter first—that of verbal dictation, or, as it is usually described, verbal inspiration.

That there were instances in which such verbal dictation found place can scarcely be doubted. The language, for instance, of direction, to Isa. 6 : 9, 10 ; Jer. 22 : 2, 3 ; Ezek. 3 : 10 ; Jer. 1 : 9, 10 ; Amos 2 : 1–10, seems to imply this; as is the case with many similar passages. If it be said that, in these cases, the truth was revealed, and the words are those of the prophet, the reply is that the account specifies words as communicated; and the most natural interpretation is that of verbal messages, with which the prophet was charged. Inspiration, therefore, in some cases, extended to the verbal form of the message. This, let us remember, did not conflict either with the free agency or individuality of the inspired man, or of those to whom he spoke. A wise human sender of a verbal message would, in doing it, so adapt his message to the individualities, both of the messenger and the recipient, as to express his meaning in the best manner possible. If this be possible, and the best course to human wisdom, it would not be less so to that which is Divine. The style of that Spirit of perfect wisdom and knowledge is a perfect one; not absolutely, or metaphysically, or rhetorically, but relatively—relatively to its recipients, and to the purpose to be accomplished.

But while there were thus undoubted examples of verbal inspiration, it cannot, therefore, be affirmed that thus it was with all. There are other recorded cases in which nothing of this kind is implied. "The hand," the power of Jehovah, is upon the prophet, and he speaks. The prophet sees a vision, and it becomes the starting-point of his prediction. Sometimes such vision is explained. Then, again, no such explanation is given. In other cases incidents are the occasion, as 2 Sam. 22; 2 Kings 19:20-34; 1 Kings 17:1-14; 21:17, 24; Obad. 1:1. Then again the impulse comes without anything outward (Acts 8:26; 10:19). "The word of the Lord came," is one form of expression employed. "The burden of the word of the Lord" is another. The connection, in these cases, rather seems to indicate the source and substance of the message than its verbal expression. Doubtless, in these cases, the influence exerted would modify and control the terms, the words of the message thus delivered. So, we may say, in that degree and respect it was verbal. Whether in rare cases we are able to think without words has been a question. Certainly, without them or without outward signs, the thinking cannot be expressed. And any powerfully controlling influence brought to bear upon the human mind and heart, as was the case with the inspired man, would also control and modify forms and manners of expression. Sometimes, in the passages above, words seem to have been used; sometimes they were only affected and controlled in the material imparted or in the manner of such impartation. The object was, of course, to secure correctness in delivery; that, as it came to the recipient, and as he delivered it, it should be the word of the Lord, and therefore a true word.

We have thus to seek some form of expression or word which will include these varied phenomena, the natural elevation, the morally sanctifying influence, the divinely spoken word, the divinely given vision or incident, the Divine impulse; and these as related to the object in view, whether of precept, prediction, rational deduction, or moral insight. "The self-same Spirit dividing to each one severally as He will," thus, "at sundry times and in divers measures," secures His purpose, the impartation of truth to man. Plenary has been suggested as best expressing it: plenary, sufficient, adequate to the end divinely proposed. In other words, we say the influence exerted, the inspiration is sufficient, adequate, to the attainment of the Divine object, that of imparting Divine truth to man ; to ensure the correct delivery of the messages of Divine dictation. This does not, of course, mean plenary as to all kinds and forms of knowledge, geological, chemical, psychological, physiological ; but so as to the Divine purpose in view. The Divine Agent, in such case, uses the imperfect vehicle of human language and human expression to make known His truth, and to convey His meaning. He is able, even through these, to accomplish His object. The message, in some cases, as in prediction, may be but imperfectly understood, both by the prophet and those to whom he speaks it. But, in its time, the full meaning can and will come out. Given the postulate of the omnipresent wisdom and knowledge of the inspiring Agent, and there can be no rational doubt or fear of His securing accurate delivery of His intended message.

If this be so, we have our definition. That of Knapp seems to meet the demand in this respect : " An extraordinary Divine influence, by which the inspired teacher was instructed, what and how he should speak in discharging the duties of his office." That of Dr. Hodge : " An influence of the Holy Spirit upon selected agents, rendering them organs of God for the infallible communication of His will ;" and that of Professor Park : " A Divine influence on the minds of the sacred writers, causing them to teach in the best possible manner whatever they intended to teach, and especially to communicate religious truth without error," are substantially the same. Here we have no attempted explanation of the phenomena. We have, however, a unifying principle, to which all such phenomena may be related, and in which they find a rational explanation.

To this have been urged various objections and difficulties. Many of them have little relevance to the real issue in this subject. They really belong to kindred topics and departments of scriptural investigation, but are not essentially involved in that of inspiration. When, for instance, difficulties are urged, in connection with uncertainties as to the text, various readings, disputed translations, or the disputed canonicity of certain books, the reply is manifest. A corrupt text, or a wrong translation, or an imperfect version, or a question of canonicity, does not at all affect the character, the authority, or inspiration of that which is pure and genuine. Inspiration is affirmed only of the genuine book, and of the pure text. Whether or not that is the case, must be decided upon historical and critical reasons and evidence.

So, too, as to the issues of fragmentary construction, say of Old Testament books; the asserted later composition, or different authorship than usually supposed, of some of these books. All these questions, it is to be said, are yet at issue. The higher scholarship is to be found on both sides. While we are told every week that it is all on one side, the next week we read a learned reply from the other. While, moreover, the old scholarship is as a unit, the new is split up into conflicting theories. But whether so or not, and however these points be decided, the books, as we now have them, whether as a whole or in parts, have received the authentication as inspired of the Master and of His apostles. "The Scripture," "the Scriptures," "the law," "the law and the prophets," "the law, the prophets, and the Psalms," and whatever their date and authorship, are thus settled by Him and them as the inspired Scriptures.

Not less direct is the reply to difficulties urged, from variations of language in quotations, by New Testament writers and speakers, from Old Testament, or that of late Old Testament writers of those that are earlier. The removal of the difficulty will come, in recognition or discovery of the purpose for which the quotation is made—the principle controlling. That principle may be sometimes that of verbal exactness, to give the very words. In others, to give only the idea or sense. Sometimes it may be as proof; sometimes to indicate only similarities, or for illustration. So again, such quotation may be from the Hebrew text, or from the Septuagint, or from an Aramaic version, or from an oral Aramaic gradually formed, and in popular usage. And then, again, from whatever version, it might have been targumed, as was by no means unusual, paraphrased in the way of explanation, as quoted. Any rational supposition, in these respects, avoids conflict in the domain of inspiration. Whatever the principle of quotation, they are always thus quoted as inspired, authoritative.

But the still further difficulty is urged from discrepancies in different accounts of the same transaction—say the death of Saul in the Old Testament, or of discourses and events in the New Testament. These, it is urged, are inconsistent with any other inspiration than that of natural or moral elevation.

Of course, if the discrepancy amount to contradiction, it is inconsistent not only with inspiration of any kind, even that which is natural, but also with historic truth. Such contradiction cannot be affirmed so long as any supposable possibility of explanation can be suggested. The discrepancy or difficulty may often be removed by reference to the specific intentions of the inspired writers or of the divinely inspiring Agent, in regard to which we are not able fully to decide. That intent may have regard, in one case, to one form of words, in another to another. In one of these cases a certain amount and arrangement of matter may have been required; in another it may have been different. Why does John omit the institution of the Lord's Supper? the agony in Gethsemane? the incident of the dying malefactor? How is it that he alone mentions that the disciples baptized? Why does Luke leave out the resurrection of Lazarus, and Matthew the parable of the prodigal son? "Ignorance has a wide range of possibilities," and any supposable hypothesis saves ignorance from contradiction. So, too, as to discrepancies as to accounts of the same transaction. "The generals of Henry the Fourth," says a living writer, "strove to tell him what passed after he was wounded at the battle of Aumale; and no two of them agreed as to the course of events which gave them the victory. Two armies beheld the battle of Waterloo; but who can tell when it began? At ten o'clock, said the Duke of Wellington; at half-past eleven, said General Alam, who rode at his side. At twelve, according to Napoleon and Davoust; and at one, according to Ney." All, perhaps, right, but each one meant a different thing or movement which he called and regarded as the beginning.

One other of these supposed difficulties claims attention: the real or supposed conflict of Scripture with secular history, or with the scientific conclusions of the past or the present century. To this the reply is twofold. Many of these mistakes and conflicts have been found to be no mistakes or conflicts, but have rather confirmed the claim of Scripture. It is to be remembered, moreover, that this language of Scripture is popular, is in the form of the contemporaneous science, whatever that was. The problem, to the inspired writer, or, rather, to the divinely inspiring Agent, was the communication of Divine truths and dealings through the medium of human language, and this in language intelligible to the actual recipients. With such an imperfect instrument the work was done. It is the business of the student and interpreter to find the Divine truth in this, its human setting; to ascertain the Divine message, or the Divine act, coming in this manner to human reception. We are constantly using words that, in their etymology, had a different meaning; that will, to speakers and hearers a century hence, be still further modified as to such meaning. We speak of natural phenomena, not in accordance with scientific accuracy; and what is now accurate will not be so fifty years hence. Chemistry now says affinity. A hundred years ago it said phlogiston. A century hence it may find a better term than either. At the same time, there is no particular difficulty in making ourselves intelligible; in making substantially correct communications.* The inspired communication, whether a precept, or a fact, or a logical conclusion, a revelation of Divine or human character, is so made as to convey its meaning—a meaning for the

---

* Professor Sanday, in his Bampton Lectures, speaks of the Traditional and the Inductive view of the Canon and Inspiration. It is to be said that there is not one of the many theories on this subject that is not traditional, that does not claim to be, and is not, to some degree, inductive. The traditional view, however, first received, is by each intelligent recipient, for himself, inductively certified. The inductive, whatever its processes of collocation and verification, starts with traditional material and preconceptions. Perhaps the distinction of historical and critical would better describe the two classes of views. And yet, the historical does not entirely leave out of view the internal and critical, and the internal and critical does not entirely ignore the external and historical. It is the undue predominance of one or the other that is to be avoided. What is needed is the full induction that will take in and fairly deal with both these forms of material; that will adjust the relative claims of each. In the confusion of recent conflict the necessity of this is becoming manifest. As it is intelligently recognized and striven for, much of this confusion will disappear. Traditional, as we shall see, has two meanings—one of these a bad one. It is, therefore, always an available ambiguity with which to discount beforehand the position of an opponent.

reader of Scripture, coming to it in earnest, truthful, prayerful examination.

Lee on Inspiration.
Jamieson on Inspiration.
Manly on Inspiration.
Charteris on Christian Scriptures.
Robson on the Bible, its Revelation, Inspiration, etc.
Hodge's discussion, and Cave on Old Testament Inspiration.

CHAPTER VI.

TRADITION, MYSTERY, MIRACLES.

Tradition.—Mystery.—Evidences of Christian Revelation.

INTIMATELY connected with the subject of the canon of Scripture, and its authority as that of an inspired revelation, is that of tradition—an authority additional, one of a different form, and coming through a different process, but originating in the same Divine source; in other words, is there a revelation and inspiration in the Church? Sometimes it may be in the line of its asserted earthly head, the successors of Peter; sometimes in the whole Church, finding expression in conciliar decision; sometimes in the concurring voice of the successive episcopate. The question, thus, is not that of historical tradition, written or otherwise. This, of course, not infallible, has its value. Our knowledge of the past, secular as well as religious, scientific as well as popular, first comes to us in that way. As it thus comes, in the first instance, it is subsequently verified, or proved to be reliable, by examination of its evidence; the reasons, in view of which others before us have given it acceptance. In this sense of the word, tradition is a source not only of information, but often of verification.

The issue, however, in this matter of tradition, as related to Scripture, or as a source of Divine information additional to Scripture, is, with reference to it in one particular form, that which is oral. The Council of Trent affirms the existence of such tradition, and places it on a level with the written Scripture. It is the divinely given and transmitted word, divinely given and preserved in oral form. There is thus, in the Church, a depositum for all ages; its infallible Head, or its infallibly directed Councils, declaring, in particular cases, and as needed, what is its substance —the material of its teaching and decisions.

To state this claim explicitly is to refute and dispose of it. There is no scriptural reason, no rational evidence outside of Scripture, by which it can be sustained. Doubtless, as St. John says, there were many sayings of our Lord that were not written in his book; and, we may add, not in any other of the Gospels. But, so far as regards the knowledge of the Church, they have passed away. Oral tradition does not even attempt to reproduce them. So with the unrecorded words and truths of apostolic preaching. No effort is made to reproduce them. Oral tradition, now, rather undertakes to say what they meant in that which is recorded. St. John, indeed, does tell of one oral tradition getting into circulation, during his time, which he corrects as giving a wrong impression. And, within the next hundred years, we find opposing views appealing to oral tradition as sustaining opposite conclusions.

The issue here is not the comparative value of truth, oral or written. Truth is truth, and has its value, however transmitted. The real issue is as to whether the oral mode is a reliable one. This, too, not only, or mainly of facts, and for short periods, but of doctrines, and for all time. The clear statement of the question suggests its answer. There is no satisfactory evidence of any such body of traditional truth beyond the lifetime of the founders of Christianity. Had any such existed, its mode of transmission would have vitiated its reliability. In such process of oral transmission it would have lost its definiteness, and gathered new and erroneous material. In closing this subject, it is well to note the ambiguity in usage as to this word tradition. A traditionalist, in one sense, is one who accepts indiscriminately what comes from the past, and without verification. In another sense, it is one who accepts oral tradition. In still another it is one who accepts knowledge and truth from the past, but verifies it by careful investigation. The word is now a favorite one with a certain class to describe any long-established opinion, with, of course, the insinuation that it has been and is thus held, simply as received and without verification. There is often a great want of truth in the terms by which men describe their opponents.

This subject fifty years ago, in the Oxford controversy, warmly contested, has largely lost its interest. The opposite extreme now is that which holds all established opinions, and from that fact, as traditional and doubtful, or at least obsolete. The subject, as between Rome and Oxford on one side, and Protestantism on the other, is exhaustively treated in Goode's "Divine Rule of Faith and Practice."

Mystery.

This, like tradition, has its connection with Scripture, and brings out the fact that in Divine revelation there are truths naturally shut, hidden from, or transcending human discovery, if not human comprehension. The word ordinarily and popularly expresses the last, that which is incomprehensible. In this sense it is frequently employed in the sacramental controversy. Thus employed, it frequently means, not an incomprehensibility, but a contradiction—as, for instance, a bodily presence, which in its very term bodily is limited, affirmed as ubiquitous, unlimited, omnipresent. Affirmations, however, without any such contradiction, may be incomprehensible. They may be apprehended as facts, as in certain of their bearings and applications. At the same time, in themselves, as in their full and ultimate explanation, they transcend all human capacity of comprehension. The Divine perfection, for instance, the Trinity in unity, the union of the Divine and human in the person of Christ, constitute illustrations of such truths. They are revealed as truths, not to be fully construed, but, in faith, accepted and followed in their practical application.

Whether the word μυστηριον is ever used in this sense in the New Testament is a matter of dispute. Predominantly its usage is different. In 1 Tim. 3:16, however, and in 1 Cor. 14:2 it rather seems to incline to this meaning. The one the great mystery of godliness before and after its revelation; the other, a man speaking in an unknown tongue, incomprehensible to his hearers. Its more frequent use is different. In such use it describes things undiscoverable in themselves, or hidden for a time from human knowledge, but in due time divinely revealed. The Gospel, in this sense, is a mystery, " the mystery hidden from ages and generations, but revealed in Christ" (1 Cor. 4:1; 15:51; Eph. 1:9; 3:3). In this sense, all truth depending for its knowledge upon Divine revelation is mystery.

But there is a still further sense in which this word is sometimes employed: to describe a truth symbolically exhibited; hidden, or secret in the symbol. This is its meaning in Eph. 5:32 and in Rev. 17:5. The great truth of the sacred union of Christ with His Church, contained, or hidden behind, symbolically exhibited in the sacred union of the wife and husband, the adulterous woman, the mystery or symbol of an apostate church. This is really its proper usage as related to the sacraments; not a contradiction, or even an incomprehensibility, but the hidden or symbolic truth in or behind the sacrament of spiritual purification with one; of spiritual loyalty, and life, and growth in the other.

This gives us the three senses of the word: (*a*) Mystery, an incomprehensibility, but not a contradiction. (*b*) Mystery, a truth needing revelation to bring it to human knowledge. (*c*) Mystery, a truth symbolically exhibited. (See Hatch, "Essays on Biblical Greek," pp. 57, 62.)

Proofs of Revelation.

We thus reach the distinct point of the proofs or evidences in view of which revelation, $\alpha\pi o\kappa\alpha\lambda v\psi\iota\varsigma$, special Divine communication, as distinct from $\varphi\alpha\nu\varepsilon\rho\omega\sigma\iota\varsigma$, natural manifestation of God to man, is believed and asserted. In Christian countries this fact is found in actual acceptance; is, so to speak, a providential inheritance. As thus preoccupying the ground, it may, from opponents, demand positive disproof of that which is thus accepted. With its recipients, and as related to its full and intelligent acceptance, it demands thorough investigation; that not only the belief itself, but the reasons and evidences in view of which it is held, should be clearly seen and exhibited. Some of these may be briefly stated:

(*a*) One of these is the character and effects of this asserted Christian revelation. "Christendom," said Coleridge, "is the argument for Christianity." The ideal Christendom would be a perfect moral demonstration. The actual, with all its defects and failures, reveals the same conclusion; still attests its Divine source and origin; what it has done and is doing in the world; what are its undoubted effects, moral, social, and spiritual, as consistently applied, and by its consistent disciples proclaims its superhuman, its Divine character. "The tree" here "is known by its fruit." Christianity, as compared with other religions, is superior in moral purity, as in spiritual and social elevation. Christianity, as compared with irreligion, is as the heavenly to the earthly. As thus such an existing world fact, of such a character, absolutely and comparatively, it demands acceptance. The alternative to that acceptance is irreligion. When it is rejected it is not for Mohammedanism, or Buddhism, or Confucianism. Whatever may be said of exceptions to this, they are so exceptional that they cannot be made an element of calculation. The alternative is Christianity or nothing; Christianity or practical atheism. To a serious, earnest man this is now the only religion. Christianity thus, in itself, in its character, its teachings and effects, as in its alternative, affords evidence of its Divine origin.

(*b*) Along with this, the essential character of Christianity, are the facts, historical and evidential, connected with its founding—the ministry and life of Christ and those of His apostles, and their immediate consequences. This ministry gathered in and organized a community largely made up of previous enemies, which has perpetuated itself, with institutions and practices that have kept it unbrokenly in public existence. The apostles testify as ear-witnesses of the Master's words, as eye-witnesses of His works and life. Their testimony is corroborated by that of other disciples contemporaneous; by that of converts, of same date, confirming thus what they had previously opposed. The rite of baptism organizing these believers into a community, the Lord's Supper a memorial of His death, the Christian Sunday taking the place of the old Sabbath as also a memorial of His resurrection—all these gave emphasis and definiteness to the events with which they were connected.

So, too, it was, in the effect of the Gospels and Epistles, as reaffirming in a written form what the Christian body, from its own knowledge, first accepted. No less significant as giving historical reality and value to this testimony of Christian believers, is that of their opponents and persecutors. All bring before us the historical fact of a new form of religious belief; this resting upon the doings and teachings and life of its Founder—these facts affirmed by eye-witnesses; accepted, as thus affirmed by contemporaries; both alike taking these asserted facts as the controlling principles of their lives—living by them, and in many cases dying for them. Such evidence, in regard to any other historical fact, would be accepted as moral demonstration.

(c) But the evidence thus far is all in the sphere of the natural. There is, further, that which is above nature, supernatural, miraculous. Supernatural sometimes means only superphysical. Here we use it in its ordinary and more extended signification. It is the extraordinary manifestation to rational beings of the presence and agency of God. It may be through natural powers and agencies, it may be with something additional; but the essential feature in it is the manifestation of Divine presence and working. This evidence, in connection with Christianity, is afforded in different forms.

(*a*) First, as its most wonderful exhibition, is that of the personality of its Founder. Jesus Christ is the miracle, the supernatural fact of human history. The most unbelieving have, in substance, over and over again admitted it. As men stand in His presence, and study His personality, and note the spirit of His life, the involuntary confession comes that here is a phenomenon without its parallel. If natural, unlike any other in the world's knowledge or experience. "Behold the Man!" You may, perhaps, deny that He wrought miracles; but you cannot deny that He is the miracle, unique, unexampled, transcendent. He is the truth. His words are certified as those of the God of truth.

(*b*) And as the personality of the Lord Jesus is thus supernatural, so it may be said is His teaching. It transcends all natural explanation of its origin. Efforts have been made to compare it with that of other religious teachers; but the effort only demonstrates the hopelessness of the comparison, the perfection above nature and beyond nature of His moral and spiritual teaching. In that teaching, as in His person, we see the supernatural, the Divine.

(*c*) Coincident with these, we may say, and included in them, are His manifestations of the supernatural in work and action. We may reverently say that such a man, such a being could not have been only natural in His words and actions. To Him the supernatural was natural. His works were those of power, exhibitive of control in the domain of physical nature. Most of them, further, were works of compassion, love, relief to the diseased and suffering. One or two, temporarily of judgment, had in view permanent results of benefit in the way of instruction; but, all alike, His works, as His teachings and person, make manifest that God was with Him. "My Father worketh, and I work," is His own declaration. The character of those works sustains His declaration: works of power controlling nature; works of love and compassion relieving natural suffering; words of knowledge revealing the future. They were thus revelations of omnipotence, of omniscience, of love. As with Nicodemus, so comes now the attestation, "No one can do," could do, "these miracles unless God were with him."

(*d*) And these miraculous powers, asserted and exercised by the Master, are by Him conferred upon and promised to the apostles; authenticated by Him as possessed by Moses and the prophets of the Old Testament. Every affirmation of revelation, a supernatural fact, implies miracle as, in some manner, involved in its bestowal.

As to the speculative difficulties in the way of the acceptance of miracles, it is to be said that, to the intelligent theist, they have no existence. They virtually rest upon the assumptions of naturalism or materialism. Human wills, for sufficient reasons, modify the course of nature and natural forces. On the grounds of naturalism we can have only natural phenomena. Bring in those that are Divine, and the results will be supernatural.

The scriptural words descriptive of miracles have their significance. One of these, δυναμις, גְּבוּרָה, expresses the truth of the Divine power put forth to its production. Another, θαυμασια, פֶּלֶא, brings out its character as wonderful and striking; as does τερας, מוֹפֵת, still more strongly; while the other two words, σημειον, אוֹת, and εργον, מִפְעָלוֹת, describe their significance and efficacy. They are exhibitions of power, wonderful, portentous signs, works of Divine origin and doing. Still further distinction has been made of miracles—ὁμο, υπο, and υπερ natural. The first, like some of the plagues of Egypt, natural as to the matter, supernatural in quantity and time, as predicted. The second, like the destruction of Sodom by volcanic action, unusual as to manner, supernatural as predicted. The last, as walking on the water; the feeding five thousand on the few loaves and fishes; the turning water into wine, above nature, in material, as in its accompaniments and precedings. In different modes, and yet alike, the Divine agency in each is exhibited.

To all these forms of evidence is added that of the correlation of the truths of revelation, with which they are connected, to the necessities and aspirations of human nature; to man as a spiritual being; as ignorant and sinful, and yet with spiritual wants, and desires, and aspirations; finding out from nature his wants, but finding no natural supply to them. The Divine Spirit in and through these truths, testifying to the human spirit, reveals the way of life, of duty, and of safety. "If any man will do the will of God, so far as that will in these truths is clear, is the assurance" he shall know further and fully. As he does, so shall he know, until, thus in doing, his knowledge is fully perfected.

The objections and difficulties as to miracles may be briefly stated.

(*a*) Miracles are impossible. This is true upon the hypothesis of atheism; but "with God all things are possible." The Author of nature, for sufficient reason, may suspend or modify the operation of natural forces.

(*b*) Miracles, if possible, are not provable. As contrary to experience, evidence cannot establish the fact of their occurrence. But evidence, in all cases, testifies to experience and its results. It thus shows that miracles are in accordance with that particular experience, and not contrary to, but only absent from other experience. The fallacy here is in the non-distribution of the middle term experience, and in the assumption that facts, not present in any particular experience, are contradicted by it.

(*c*) Miracles, or the facts called miracles, are possible and provable, but have not been, and are not proved. But, if admitted to be provable, the actual evidence afforded in character and degree, is all that could be asked or gotten, for any fact of human acceptance and belief. Further, when it is said, "not proved," the question, in reply, may be, "not proved" to whom? The proof has been accepted as satisfactory by men of every order and class of mind, of cultivation, and of character—Newton, Brewster, Arnold, Guizot, the African, the Hottentot, the Indian. What men, of every class, and century after century, accept must be regarded as proved. Proof is not apt to convince opponents who have assumed their position.

(*d*) Miracles are possible and provable, and, perhaps, have taken place ; but, if it can be done, they must be regarded as natural. Here we have the naturalistic explanations : " Quickened process of nature" (Olshausen) ; " increased nourishing power of the bread" (Lange) ; " words of Jesus, misunderstood in the storm" (Paulus) ; " the calm faith of Jesus when the helmsman despaired of safety" (Schenkel) ; " a symbol of analogous mental phenomena" (Schleiermacher).

" Let the account stand," says Luthardt, in opposition to all this—" let the account stand as it reads." " It is idle, and worse—cowardly," says Dr. Thompson, " to withhold our faith in a Bible miracle until we can find or invent some way in which the thing may have happened, without any great miracle after all."

The truth, exaggerated and caricatured in most of these objections, is, that miracle, as unusual and extraordinary, demands extraordinary evidence. That evidence has been and is afforded. The establishment, moreover, of one or two central miracles, say that of the giving of the law at Sinai of the Old Testament, or of the resurrection of our Lord in the New Testament, makes credible many of a subordinate character.

CHAPTER VII.

THE DOCTRINE OF GOD.

The idea and its definitions.—Forms of Scriptural statement.—The two kinds of proof of Divine existence.—Forms of unbelief as to this truth.

The transition is natural from revelation to its Author, and central truth: the Being, in this revelation, making Himself known to men. "In the beginning God" is the opening sentence in that revelation—"in the beginning God." The word, in its etymology, expresses one of His attributes—that of goodness—that His existence and working blesses His creatures. The question has been further asked, Can there be any word, any definition of Him in His essential being and character? Here, as in other things, we need bear in mind that exhaustive definitions are difficult, if not impossible. We have to content ourselves with those that are differentiative; that distinguish the object from all others. This meets the necessity of human thought, as it is the limit of human capacity. "You may," says a living writer,* "deny the idea of the Infinite as not clear; and clear it is not if nothing but the mental picture of an outline deserve that word,

* James Martineau.

But if a thought is clear which sets apart, without danger of being confounded with another, when it can exactly keep its own in speech and reasoning, without forfeit and without encroachment—if, in short, logical elements consist, not in the idea of a limit, but in the limit of the idea, then no sharpest image of any finite quantity is clearer than the thought of the Infinite." This thought goes into every such definition. The " I am" of Ex. 3 : 14, the self-existent being, the source of all other beings, would be an illustration. "The most perfect being, and the source of all others, brings out the feature of moral perfection as of self-sufficiency. This perfection is not only related to its objects, but absolute in its essential character and attributes.

At the same time, and in connection with passages of this character, are others predominantly speaking of God in His relations ; in the perfection of those relations to His creatures. He thus makes Himself an intelligible object of contemplation to His creatures. He reveals Himself as Creator, Preserver, Provider, Benefactor, and Supreme Ruler ; adapts Himself to their capacity of comprehension. Every such relation, moreover, is not only intelligible, but practical ; makes its demand upon human dependence as upon human affection and obligation. " Jehovah is the true God ; He is the everlasting King. He hath made the earth by His power, He hath established the world by His wisdom, and hath stretched out the heaven by His discretion" (Jer. 10 : 10, 12). "God that made the world, and all things therein" (Acts 17 : 24). " Which made the heaven, and earth, the sea, and all that therein is: which keepeth truth forever" (Ps. 146 : 6). So too Isa. 42 : 5 ; 45 : 6, 7. He thus describes Himself as not only the Infinite, the Self-Existent, but as the Creator, Governor, Preserver, and Benefactor of all His creatures ; as the Father of these His creatures, of all intelligent, rational, and spiritual beings.

Proofs of Divine Existence.

In the discussion of this subject two perfectly distinct questions are frequently confounded. One of these is, How do we actually get this idea or truth of God—of the Divine existence and personality? Another is, How can this idea or truth, and, in whatever way gotten, be rationally verified, shown to be true? To validate, for instance, the cosmological or teleological argument, it is not necessary that it be affirmed as previously involved in acts of consciousness ; as, on the other hand, the denial of the derivation of this truth from consciousness does not interfere with conclusions from any of these others. As to the first of these questions, How do we actually get our knowledge of this truth? it must be said that, like those to whom the Old and New Testament Scriptures were given, we find ourselves, prior to all proof, in actual possession. We have received it by inheritance from our Christian parents, as they did from their patriarchal ones. Whether it has ever been received in any other way may well be a question. With those who have lost, or obscured it by retrogression into conditions of lowest savageism, the tendency is to go lower, not higher. If they get or recover it, it is brought to them by the civilized missionary or teacher. Theistic peoples, monotheistic peoples especially, as a matter of fact, before they verify this truth, get it from those preceding them. And the most rational supposition, in view of all the facts of the case, is that of primæval revelation. It has been easy to imagine, and we have all read descriptions of the process and stages by which the ape, rising into the stone man, and the stone man into the iron man, and the iron man into the hunter, and the hunter into the grazier and tiller of the soil, and the tiller of the soil into the citizen, the enlightened, moral, and spiritual Christian. But the actual facts do not correspond. Below the condition of the first men in Genesis—that of tillers of the soil—the tendency is to go lower, not higher. But whether thus or not, the question of the proof of this is one of a different character. So, too, in reference to the assertion that God is known in the action of consciousness; that the self-consciousness of the dependent ego is the natural condition to the knowledge of the All-Sufficient source of dependence; or that human nature is so constituted that the idea, however presented, validates itself as a reality. Still all this is distinct from the proof of the truth thus accepted. As a matter of fact, we have it. How is it verified?

Here we have the old division of the proofs, *a priori* and *a posteriori*. The former of these—the *a priori* of one kind—is that from cause to effect, or from reason to consequent; of another is that from *a priori* truths, or intuitions, necessarily given as the occasion is presented. The argument of Anselm, from the idea of perfect being, as a cause or reason, to infer actual existence an effect, included in that idea or cause, is an illustration of the former. On the principle of Anselm's realistic philosophy, that to every idea there was a reality; that the logical and ontological existences were identical, this argument was a valid one. On any other it is defective; has never been accepted as satisfactory.

The other form of this *a priori* argument is that from *a priori* truths or necessary intuitions. The idea of perfect or infinite being, it is affirmed, is a necessity of human thought; and as thus a rational necessity, must be accepted as true. Think space, and you cannot avoid thinking infinite space. Think time, and you cannot avoid thinking infinite duration. Think being, and you necessarily think infinite being. Whether the step in this last, being, is immediate as with space and time, has been a question. With Clarke the intermediate was the necessity of substance, or being, as necessarily implied in these of space and time; with others this intermediate is the causal idea—finite being demanding that of the infinite to account for its existence. This last, however, brings it within the domain of the *a posteriori*, from effect to cause. Taking this causal idea, the argument is a valid one. That which comes to us as a necessity of human thought, and which comes as a reality, must be accepted.

Kant's distinction of speculative and practical reason, as vitiating this conclusion, cannot be sustained.

Whatever the value of this argument, one of its results passes over for further use. It validates the truth of infinitude in space and time directly, if not in being; of infinitude in being as the necessary causal ground of finite being. We pass on to the other class of proofs, the *a posteriori*.

(*a*) One of these has been called that of contingency, revealed in the fact of changes in the world, of matter, and of existence; of things beginning to be and coming to certain forms of termination. The finite, the dependent, the changeable, find their explanation in something preceding and continuing. This, whether regarded as a force or a personality, is immeasurable, especially as we take in the immensity of the known universe. As, moreover, we know and can only conceive of one kind of originating efficient, that of will of personality, we find in this, in infinite, will and personality, an intelligible and sufficient explanation of the world, in its existence and changes. Any other hypothesis fails to meet the demands of the problem. To the counter assertion that effects and causes are only antecedents and consequents, the reply is that we know them, in ourselves, as different. We ourselves are efficient causes, and our actions and their results are consequences and effects. What we thus know in ourselves we transfer to other personalities.

(*b*) Connected with this, and bringing in an additional feature, is the cosmological argument. This finds the world of beginnings and changes not a chaos, but a cosmos, an orderly arrangement, relations of parts to each other, of parts to a whole, of these several wholes to unifying principles—to a few, or, it may be, one such principle by which all is pervaded. The argument is thus, not only from change, beginnings, but of order, of intelligent arrangement, needing intelligence to account for it. Here, also, in view of the extent or the arrangement and of the variety of the materials, is the demand for intelligence of infinite capacity.

(c) An advance upon this, in degree if not in kind, is the teleological—that which finds not only changes and order, as in the two preceding, but also such order and arrangement as conduce to the attainment of certain ends or purposes. Sometimes, for instance, structures are so related, in their respective parts, to a unified whole; and these wholes to others, as to their surroundings and necessities of perpetuation, of existence and enjoyment, that purpose is manifested in them. As they are, and as they are related, they manifestly have ends in view. There is purpose indicated in their existence. The eye is for seeing, the ear for hearing, as with numberless cases of similar character. Such purpose is manifest, supposing to every such structure a distinct origin, and perpetuated without change from the first creation. But it is no less manifest, supposing it the effect of numberless changes by which these forms of structure gradually passed into others. The fact, whether by a leap or by a long process of preparation, is the same fact; and in it are the same indications of purpose. It rather, indeed, increases the evidence of wisdom, and skill, and purpose in the complicated and progressive stages through which the result is reached. Evolution demands involution, the plan and purpose under which it begins and goes on to its result. In it, as in the creation of the world, as it actually is, are marks of design, purpose, teleology. An intelligence of infinite capacity, a will of infinite resources is needed for its realization. Of course, indications in this cosmos of wisdom, of goodness, increase the evidence as to the perfection of its Author; moral, as well as intellectual perfection. Objection to this or that particular, as involving pain and suffering, may be urged. But even in many of these there is revelation of higher benefit; and the general purpose and predominant effect of good may be easily recognized.*

(*d*) To this has been added what has been called the anthropological: the indications, as in the others, of

---

* Difficulties have been made, in connection with this argument of design or purpose, in the phenomena of nature. One has been specially insisted upon: that the idea of design goes with us in the investigation; consequently we do not find it in the phenomena. But this is to confound two things perfectly distinct. The idea of design in its origin is, with man, a designing being. If he were not so he could never be able to find or even comprehend it. This idea, which he gets in the first movements of his own mind, he takes with him into the investigation of phenomena; and in such phenomena recognizes its existence and presence. I, as a designing, purposing being, recognize such design and purpose, teleological results made manifest in things around me.

beginnings, of order, of purpose; but all these heightened and increased in the phenomena of human nature, as related, in its organic being, to the world and its surroundings; as, in its rational, moral, and spiritual constitution, related to a moral and spiritual order, and to its Divine Author. Here we have personality in its capacities of being and of doing; and in such personality is proof of that of its Author. The fact reveals the nature of its cause. Personal being is the only adequate, as a cause, to personal being. Man, created in the image of God, is thus a revelation of his personal Creator.

(e) With all these comes in, and upon its own specific evidence, that of revelation, with its miraculous attestation. God, in that revelation, not only makes known His will, but gives increased and co-operative proof of His existing presence, and power, and perfection. Specially is this the case in His dealings with His ancient people; in His interpositions for their benefit or correction. Peculiarly is this proof afforded in His predicted purposes, as in the progress of ages they have been verified. God, as working and speaking, and in these special modes, manifests alike His existence and His perfection. Of course, not so much from particular texts as from facts of His dealing are to be found God's manifestations of Himself, not only to His people, but to all men and in all coming ages.

How I first got that idea has nothing to do with the rational conviction of its presence and reality. For full investigation of this subject, see Jackson's prize essay, "Philosophy of Natural Theology."

These different proofs are usually thought of as identical. There is really in them the element of progress. In each there is an advance upon those preceding. In that of contingency, for instance, is the truth of an originating Intelligence and Power, and this all pervasive. In the cosmological are these forces of intelligence and power in an orderly manner, and in manifold operation. In the teleological is, further, the purpose and design, additional, over all and in all, to the attainment of certain results, manifestive of infinite knowledge, wisdom, and benevolence. Last of all, in the anthropological is found the image of the Divine Original, rationally necessitating the existence of that Original. And, corroborative of all, and with additional evidence, is that of specific revelation.

Unbelief as to the Divine Existence.

Contrasted with this truth of God, accepted and verified in the forms indicated, is that first and most sharply of atheism. This, in its form of statement, is negative; and the $\alpha\theta\epsilon o\iota$ of Eph. 2:12 and of Ps. 53:1 were rather the godless, the practical, than the theoretic or dogmatic atheists. It is sometimes asserted that atheism is impossible, usually upon the assumed postulate that human nature, mediately or immediately, knows God and cannot help knowing Him. Even, however, upon this postulate, is to be borne in mind the capacity in human nature of resisting and overcoming natural convictions, of obscuring rational intuitions. And, whether it be accepted or not, over against this assertion is the undoubted historical fact that such belief has been explicitly avowed—dogmatic atheism. This, as the affirmation of a negative, can only be established by an exhaustive analysis of the contents of the universe; is, rationally, a hopeless undertaking. The affirmation of atheism demands the capacity of Omniscience, which implies God. It is sufficient, for our purpose, simply to indicate what may be regarded as the forms of atheism.

(*a*) The dogmatic, that which positively affirms it.

(*b*) The speculative, which fails to find proof of its opposite.

(*c*) The practical, which, perhaps accepting it, the truth of God, acts and lives as if it were false.

With this subject of atheism is usually connected that of pantheism, the belief or form of philosophy which identifies the Divine and cosmical existence. That of Spinoza, of one substance, with its two principles, or attributes of thought and extension, variously modified, is that which is best known. Later systems in Germany have involved additional modifications. Perhaps the simplest distinction in this matter is that of materialistic and idealistic pantheism. With the former, matter in its simplest element is the point of departure. Deity, intelligence, Divine and human alike, as everything intermediate, is an evolution from matter in its simplest principle; Deity, however, in some manner present with matter in its initiative as in its continuative potentialities. With the latter, taking mind as the point of departure, the world is an emanation of Deity; at the same time is in Deity, as Deity is in it. Practically, with the average man, the first of these is atheism, and the last frequently runs into it. The results of both are fatalistic, logically destructive of personality; consequently of accountability, as of the springs of human exertion and aspiration.

Allied to these forms of speculative and practical unbelief, as to the Divine existence and perfection, are two others of comparatively modern origin and prevalence—those of positivism and agnosticism. The principle of the former, positivism, is that of positive or real knowledge as confined to the domain of physical science, or facts verifiable by the senses. Ethics, psychology, and theology are thus ruled out, as not authorized to make affirmations of a scientific or positive character. The progress of the race has been, first, the theological, in its successive stages of fetichism, polytheism, monotheism; the metaphysical, or stage of doubt; the positive, that of certified knowledge. Religion is a matter of feeling. The object to which it is directed cannot be proved to exist. The later course of Comte was strangely inconsistent with some of these features of his system. But, to all intents and purposes, positivism is practical atheism.

Agnosticism, in contrast with this, affirms the necessity of a sufficient ground for the existence of the universe, an originating efficient; but it denies that affirmation can be made as to attributes or modes of operation. We thus know the world, and, in our knowledge of this world, know necessarily of its Author. But as to His character, and dealings, and relations to men, and of His principles of operation, we are ignorant. The altar, if erected, is to the unknown God.

Two other terms need brief explication.

Deism, simple in its etymology, but in its usage better described by the word naturalism; the equivalent, also, of what is usually spoken of as rationalism. It accepts the truth of a God as known in nature and as Creator; but it excludes the truth of His continued personal action, of providential control, and presence, and interposition in nature. All forces and agencies, as originally set in operation, unvaryingly continue, are natural.

Theism, the same word in its Greek form, has a much more expanded significance. It is often the equivalent of deism; so, again, of agnosticism; at the same time, by others is applied to Christianity. Any form of belief in this modern usage, accepting the idea or truth of God, is theism. It needs, therefore, to be used carefully and with discrimination. The speaker may mean Christianity; the hearer may understand it as naturalism or agnosticism.

Harris's " Philosophical Basis of Theism."
Hodge, Charles, " Theology," 1 vol.
Hetherington's " Apologetics."
Steenstra's " The Being of God as Unity and Trinity."
" Discourse Concerning the Being and Attributes of God," by Samuel Clarke.
Dorner's " Theology."

CHAPTER VIII.

THE DIVINE ATTRIBUTES.

Grounds of conception as to these.—The two features of Scriptural teaching.—Attributes of Personality.—Divisions of them.—Divine Unity, Spirituality, Eternity, Omnipotence, Omniscience, Omnipresence, Holiness, Truth, Justice, Wisdom and Love, or Goodness.

In any endeavor to apprehend or get ideas of the perfections of God, we find our limit in our own capacities. These, while helping us, at the same time do not, in their results, fully give what we are seeking. They are, however, our highest and fullest source of comprehension and of information; analogically enable us to understand the Divine character and perfections. We get our ideas of those perfections as they are outwardly manifested in nature. We are told of them in the revelations of Scripture. And, from nature within, from our own intellectual, moral, and spiritual personalities, evidence corroborative and elucidative is afforded. We know ourselves as personalities, intelligent, rational, volitional; capable of selecting ends, adapting means to their attainment; knowing them as morally good and evil. Man is thus higher than the mere vital, physical, or instinctive capacity. All these he includes in himself; and he is, additionally, much more and higher. We take him, the highest of all earthly creatures; and take that in him which elevates him above these, as affording the clearest and fullest evidence of the perfections of his Divine Author. In so doing, we endeavor to remove all human imperfections, to heighten all human excellence; in this manner, to get an intelligible and worthy, although it may be an inadequate knowledge, of the Divine Being and character. Anthropomorphisms, however imperfect or liable to perversion, are less so than any other. The alternative, too, is to something lower. We cannot avail ourselves of angelomorphisms, for these, when intelligible, are anthropomorphic. Efforts to avoid this—in other words, to construe the world and its Divine Author under the morphisms of gravity, affinity, vitality—are at the bottom of much of the scepticism of our day. If any of these give an idea of God, it will be that of a being, as simply an immense, unintelligent force, ceaselessly operating. He, or it, while perhaps dreaded, cannot be an object of love, of obedience, or devotion. Instinctive, vital, affinitive, or atomic cannot therefore be depended upon to save us from the dangers of anthropomorphism. In the human personality is the analogy, the image of the Divine.

It is well worthy of note that inspired teaching seems to anticipate and guard against the danger, alike, of anthropomorphic and abstract conceptions. The former, unmingled, would tempt to only human conceptions of Deity; the latter, if alone, would be unintelligible. Its declarations at times speak of the

Infinite, the Eternal, the Self-Existent, the Immutable. At other times He is described as speaking and doing, as pleased and displeased, as grieved or gratified in the actions of His creatures. He is thus God in the infinitude of His perfections ; that perfection including His interest and presence, and dealings with all of His dependent creatures.

With this central truth, therefore, of personality, we begin in our efforts to see His attributes or perfections. The Divine Being or nature we may say is the sum of these perfections. These enable us to know His working, the principles controlling. Various divisions of these have been made ; such, for instance, as negative and positive—the negative, in which we remove all imperfections that are in ourselves, as those of knowledge, in Omniscience ; the positive, in which we add such qualities, as perfect justice and goodness, to ours imperfect. Further, the division of active and passive attributes, justice and omnipotence of the active, eternity and omnipresence of the passive. Still further is the division of the natural or physical and the moral ; the latter those in which there is the exercise of the Divine will, as, for instance, justice as distinguished from knowledge or power, in which will is not included. All these divisions are defective ; but the last is the simplest and least liable to objection. The words physical and natural have, indeed, in later usage, become materialized in their association. It is difficult to find a substitute. Perhaps dynamical or substantial might be taken.

Divine Unity.

Carrying, therefore, with us, in our examination of each of these attributes, the truth of personality, we look first at those which are natural as distinguished from moral; and as unifying our view of their character and operation, single or combined, we first contemplate the truth of the Divine unity. The proof of this is twofold: first, in the idea of infinite perfection, which cannot be conceived of but as one. Division implies capacity of addition, as of further division, and thus voids the idea of infinitude. So, in the calling into existence of the world, its preservation and government, unity alone meets all the demands of the problem, and settles it without complication. It is to be said that the clear recognition of the Divine personality is usually connected with that of the unity. In polytheistic religions there is apt to be confusion as to both.

The scriptural enunciation of this truth is clear, distinct, and emphatic. It was the one point in which the religion of Israel was Protestant against the world—the point of their temptation to individual and national apostasy—and, therefore, one in which they received full instruction. "Hear, O Israel! Jehovah our God is one Jehovah" (Deut. 6:4). "To us," says the apostle, "there is one God" (1 Cor. 8:4, 6). "I am God, and there is none else" (Isa. 45:5, 21, 22). "Thou art God alone" (Ps. 86:10). To these may be added others. See especially Deut. 4:35-39; 32:39.

Intimately connected, in the way of contrast, with this truth of the Divine unity, is that of the existence and prevalence of its opposite, polytheism, many gods; sometimes that of a monarchy, with one superior; sometimes that of superior and inferior classes; sometimes if not exactly equal, yet singly exerting power and objects of dread and worship. The problem has been its origin. The apostle, in Rom. 1:19, 23, finds it in neglect and perversion of divinely given truths and evidences as to the true God in the beginning. This accords with the Old Testament in its historical dealing with it, as in its constant reprobation of it. The first men are monotheists. Enoch walked with God; Noah's loyalty to God is emphasized; and Abraham seems to have been called in his own life witness, as in the existence of his descendants, to perpetuate it in the world, as to protest against its opposite.

Accordant with this is the fact that, in the religions of the world, the earliest stages are the purest; the grosser forms of polytheism come later. The personification of Divine attributes or of natural powers was perhaps the first stage; the worship of the attribute or power thus personified in due time following; the deification of human powers, or humanity, one of its last stages. However begun, it rapidly spread; and in the time of Abraham seems to have reached a point at which a special dispensation was needed to preserve and perpetuate the primitive truth, from which it was a departure. It is further to be said of polytheism that while it sometimes gave so much prerogative to one of its deities that it bordered on monotheism, in another, it so identified all the deities with the powers and operations of nature, that it becomes pantheism. The gross polytheism of the multitude was the pantheism of philosophers. At different stages one or other of these, holding in solution its opposite, openly predominated; but rarely, if ever, rising into consistent monotheism. Historically exhibited, and impressed upon God's chosen people through their long experience, it became to them a permanent possession; and, through them, has been inherited by the world. The effort to evolve monotheism from fetichism, through the lower forms of polytheism, and from these through the higher forms of polytheism, is one that breaks down at every stage of its undertaking.*

* Perhaps, as striking illustration of the hopelessness of such attempt, is that afforded by Dr. Matheson in his "Messages of the Old Religions." Starting with the assumption of fetichism—that is, religion, an evolution from and through the lower up to the highest—he exhibits this rising progress. The oldest religion—not that of Adam or Abel, but of men without knowledge or idea of God—begins in its process with one of the lowest objects, say, a stone or piece of wood, this having or giving to man the consciously changing being, the idea of permanence. Attaining in the stone this idea of permanence, he manages to transfer it to himself by the dream experience. As he finds that he continues through the dreaming and waking state the same being, so, like the stone, he is immortal. The next stage, it may be, is the spiritualizing the fetich, the stone, by carving or making it like a man. This may be idolatry; but, according to the author, it is not polytheism. "Polytheism," he tells us, "is impossible. There never really existed or could exist a time in which the mind of man had its attention simultaneously fixed upon two objects of worship." Perhaps not, or upon any other two things. But how as to different times? Polytheism is not the simultaneous worship of different deities, but of these deities at different times, and in different acts of devotion. The heroes of Homer did not worship Zeus, or Neptune, or Apollo in the same time

Spirituality of God.

"*Unus vivus, et verus Deus*" ("the true God, one and living") is the opening sentence of our first article. The unity and living personality of the Divine Being thus stand first, in point of contemplation, in any endeavor to know or exhibit His attributes or perfections. This, of unity, goes with us in all that follows, and enables us to see it in its full significance. "The Lord our God," a sentence to be read on the walls of many Jewish synagogues, as the great truth of that dispensation—"the Lord our God is one Lord."

With this truth of the Divine unity, thus to be taken with us, and implied in all the Divine perfections, is another—that of the Divine infinitude: God as infinite, not subject to limitation in space, or capacity of being or of action. This truth, like that of Divine unity, goes into and is implied in the exercise of all His attributes. It is thus, to use the idea of Dr. Fairchild, not so much a Divine attribute as the mode of all His attributes. In all these, natural and moral alike, in being, and counselling, and doing, He is infinite.

and act, as do not those now who worship the Virgin, the saint, or the ascended Master. This theory of Henotheism, the worship of all in one, or of one in all, is a generalization and abstraction of which the primitive man was hardly capable, and which it would be difficult, if not impossible, to verify in the phenomena of any historical religion. If we could discover a colony of respectable Henotheists, there might be some hope of tracing it to its origin. So, too, as to all those hypotheses, which derive the idea of God from dreams, from animism, or personification, or self-deification, or fear, or self-deception. They do not rest, to use the language of another, upon any basis of established truth—cannot be verified.

Nothing short of this meets the necessity of human thought in the question of an originating and adequate Cause of the finite world and its phenomena. In the infinitude of the one personal God is the solution, and the only satisfactory solution, of the problem of the world, as of its beings and forms of existence.

But this infinite Being is especially to be contemplated as an infinite Spirit. As Spirit, He is not related to space or to any point or duration of time; not thus, in space, not included in any extent of duration. As Spirit, He is intelligent, moral, and free. As perfect Spirit, He is perfect in each of these respects. Matter and animal force operate, or are set in operation, through material or organic forces; spirit, by intelligence and will. In the idea, therefore, of perfect Spirit is that of perfect intelligence, perfection of purpose as of will, in counsel and in action. We, as finite spirits, act upon each other and the world through mediate agencies; God, as infinite, perfect Spirit, immediately and perfectly. "God is a spirit" (Ex. 20 : 4; Col. 1 : 15; 1 Tim. 1 : 17; Isa. 46 : 5; John 4 : 24).

From this there are several scriptural inferences.

(*a*) Worship to God must be not merely outward, but the outward must be the movement and expression of the inward "in spirit and in truth."

(*b*) Such worship cannot be exclusively localized. Where the human spirit really worships, the Divine Spirit is present to accept and bless it.

(*c*) As Spirit, He cannot be represented in any visible image or figure.

(*d*) These representations, as imperfect, lead to wrong and degrading ideas of His personality, eventually to polytheism, and are, therefore, forbidden. This is the prohibition of the second commandment—the sin of the calves, in the wilderness, and that of Jeroboam. Ahab's sin, the worship of Baal, in opposition to that of Jehovah, was more daring, a violation of the first commandment. How far possible, in Christian worship, is one of the problems of our time.

Eternity of God.

This is, of course, involved in the idea of infinite perfect Being. As perfect Spirit, unrelated in existence to periods of duration, He is eternal. The eternity thus spoken of is absolute both as to the past and as to the future. We predicate eternal life, as does Scripture, of beings who come into existence; who begin to be, but to whose existence there is no ending. The eternal life of such a being begins, and endlessly continues. The eternal life of God has no such beginning; is so from eternity to eternity. "He is the same." In the perfection of that eternal and immutable existence is the necessary ground of that of the universe, as of all His creatures.

In this truth, moreover, of the eternity of the infinite perfect Spirit, is that of His immutability. As His years have no beginning nor ending, so is He in the unchangeableness of His perfection. As His purposes are grounded in the perfections of His being, so are they without change or variation. He is, thus, self-existent, has the ground of His existence in Himself and prior to all other beings and things; is independent, uncontrolled by any of these His dependent creatures. Passages exhibiting this attribute are Isa. 44:6; 41:4: "I am the first and the last, and beside Me there is no God." "I am Jehovah, the first and the last, calling the generations from the beginning." Ps. 90; Heb. 1:10: "Thou Lord in the beginning hast laid the foundations of the earth." "Thou art the same." "They shall change, but Thou remainest." 1 Tim. 6:16: "Who only hath immortality." Rom. 1:20: "His eternal power and Godhead." 2 Pet. 3:8: "One day is with the Lord as a thousand years." Heb. 6:17: "The immutability of His counsel." Mal. 3:6: "I, Jehovah, change not." James 1:17: "Without variableness, or shadow of turning." Ps. 33:11: "The thoughts of His heart are to all generations." Rom. 11:33-36: "Of Him, and through Him, and to Him are all things."

Under this attribute are two difficulties needing examination. One of these is the class of passages in which God is spoken of as repenting, as grieved, as changing His purposes. These are to be regarded as anthropomorphisms, and anthropopathisms, in which God, speaking after the manner of men, and describing His actions, like those of men, dictated by certain affections and feelings. These, like passages which speak of God as with human organs, as with hands, or an arm, or with ears, are accommodations to human conception, and to be explained in the light of those preceding.

So, too, as to one of the words used to describe endless duration, עוֹלָם and αιων. Their significance, it may be said, is the duration of which the being, or thing spoken of, is capable. The עוֹלָם or αιων, or age, of an individual, it may be, is sixty or eighty years; that of a generation is between thirty and forty; that of the race is longer, that of the planet is longer still; that of God with no beginning nor end. The connection, therefore, must, and usually without difficulty does settle, in what sense it is to be taken. Κοσμος it has been said, is the world projected in space, as αιων is this world projected in time—that is, world in duration. At the same time, as applied to God, it may be eternity absolute; applied to men, it may be eternity relative; with beginning, but with no end.

OMNIPOTENCE OF GOD.—In the perfection of infinite Spirit is the attribute of power. This, while contemplated in its results and operations as physical, is the exercise of moral and spiritual perfection—the outgoing of the Divine will. Omnipotence has been defined the power of doing all things possible, or whatever God wills. Impossibilities to Almighty Power are contradictions. "Such contradictions," to use the language of Dr. Sparrow, "may relate to the object or the agent. An object may imply it immediately and openly, or consequentially and covertly. That a thing should be and not be is an example of the first, which, in its statement, contradicts itself. That a thing should be in two places at the same time is an example of the second, the covert and the consequential.

This latter may be resolved, after proceeding one step, into the former. So as to the agent. An action implies contradiction to God, as an Agent, when it is repugnant to His essential perfections. On this ground it is no derogation of Him to say that He cannot cease to exist, or want, or do evil, as these would imply that He was not God. "With Him all things are possible," and yet "He cannot look upon iniquity but with abhorrence." His omnipotence is that of rational and moral perfection; of course in the operation of natural forces and laws as of special and supernatural interposition.

This attribute is exhibited in Scripture figuratively and literally. "By the word of Jehovah were the heavens made, and all the host of them by the breath of His mouth" (Ps. 33 : 6, 9). "The hand of Jehovah is not shortened" (Isa. 59 : 1). "Our God is in heaven: He doeth whatsoever He will" (Ps. 115 : 3). "Calling things that are not as things that are" (Rom. 4 : 17). "Thou hast made the heaven and earth by Thy power and outstretched arm" (Jer. 32 : 17). "By Thy will Thou hast created all things" (Rev. 4 : 11 ; Job 38).

OMNISCIENCE OF GOD.—This, as the attributes already mentioned, is included in the idea of perfect Spirit, infinite personality. Spirit, as Spirit, is intelligent; perfect Spirit is all knowing, is omniscient. The knowledge thus predicated as Divine is analogous in certain respects to that which is human; and yet in others transcends all human comparison or comprehension. Human knowledge is of the present and the past, but of both imperfectly. The future can only be conjectured; and of its real connection with the present and the past we are profoundly ignorant. Omniscience includes all these, and perfectly. We know them only as under temporal conditions; as known in the present, as remembered from the past, or as anticipated for the future. To omniscience—from eternity to eternity—they are known and fully comprehended. "From the beginning of the world, known unto God are all His works" (Acts 15:18). Transcending, as it does, the capacity of human thought to its comprehension, it is a necessity of such thought, in this truth of spiritual perfection.

As this truth is of constant practical interest, it is frequent in scriptural affirmation. In the perfection of His knowledge God comprehends Himself, and in all the perfections of His being. Finite spirits fail to know themselves, fail and fall short at the highest in their knowledge of God. He knows both—Himself, in His perfection; man, in his imperfection. In His knowledge are included all beings and all things, their powers and operations, their results in human action; in the consequences of such action; in the possibilities and probabilities of human volition. "To the eye of Him all things are naked and opened" (Heb. 4:13). "He clothes the lilies, upholds the sparrows; knows man's necessities of food and raiment; tries the reins and the heart of men; knows their thoughts." "His eyes are over the righteous, and His ear open to their cry, and His face is against them that do evil"

(Matt. 6 : 26–32 ; Jer. 11 : 18–20 ; Ps. 94 : 9, 10, 11 ; 139 ; 1 Pet. 3 : 12).

Connected with this attribute, in its exercise, have arisen certain speculative difficulties. One of these is as to the mode of such exercise, whether, in it, is involved the element of succession. Secondly, as to the possibilities of Divine knowledge, extending to results contingent upon human action ; and, therefore, sometimes not actually taking place. And, last, as to the relation of Divine knowledge and foreordination to human freedom and accountability. We take them in the order presented. As to the first, the mode of the Divine knowledge, the reply is that it transcends all finite comprehension. Finite human knowledge, as we have seen, is related to the past, the present, and the future, remembrance, experience, anticipation ; the element of succession, from one of them to the other. We not only thus know, under the limitations of time, but, in our thoughts and forms of expression as to Divine knowledge, and only as making it comprehensible, we use the same terms. At the same time, in perfect knowledge, such limitation is excluded. That knowledge, however, thus from eternity to eternity, is no less through, and in all time, ever cognizant, and of everything. It includes things as they are contemplated, and as they actually are ; as they take place, and as related to their agents, their accompaniments, and their consequences.

So, too, as to the question of knowledge, with reference to events contemplated, that do not actually take place. The incident of David at Keilah (1 Sam. 23 : 11, 12), and of St. Paul in the shipwreck (Acts 27 : 22, 31), are illustrations. The reply is simple. Perfect knowledge comprehends not only actual results, events, and forms of action, but the results of different modes of proposed action. Human capacity is often able thus to foresee; much more that which is Divine.

The only difficulty in this last, however, is involved in the third—that they are foreknown, and therefore absolutely, unconditionally foreordained. Foreknowledge, in such case, is made the equivalent of foreordination, and this as unconditional. What is foreknown, it is argued, must take place, and therefore cannot be free. But foreknowledge, if perfect, as must be that of Omniscience, foreknows the action as that of a free action; any ordination is in view of that feature in it as of all others. Foreknowledge is not the ground of the act. The act, contemplated and known as a free act, is the ground of the foreknowledge. The unconditional is in the world of physical and mechanical forces and operations; the conditional always in that of moral and spiritual, and, therefore, accountable agency.

Election and Foreordination.

Under this attribute of perfect Divine knowledge usually comes up the question of election and foreordination. As in the domain of the Infinite, the subject has its difficulties. These have been greatly complicated in the manner and spirit in which the controversy in regard to them has gone on. Two classes of those difficulties need to be considered—those of a philosophical and those of a scriptural character. The philosophical are involved in the effort to construe the idea of perfect eternal knowledge with those of fore, and present, and after; as also of any decree of election or foreordination, having no regard to the actions or character of the individuals or classes thus decreed. If, however, the Divine knowledge be eternally perfect, it must include everything, all action and all character. And individuals must be contemplated, and as they really are, as the objects of Divine determination.

The scriptural difficulties have largely risen from the failure to note the variations of meaning in the words elect, predestinate, etc. Sometimes, for instance, they describe an outward condition of reception of Divine blessing. Sometimes the inward state of those morally responding to these facts of their condition. In the first of these senses all Israel was the elect. In the second, it was really only the obedient, loyal portion to Jehovah. The election in both cases was to present blessing; to its enjoyment and improvement; to higher blessing as the result of that improvement; to the duty of communicating those blessings to others. Just as was the individual response at any one of these stages, so was the election made effectual. When that response was wanting, the election as to inward blessing was made void. While of Divine grace at every such stage, in its origination as in its final heavenly result, it was only in the response of human faith that such grace became effectual. It is of faith that it may be by grace. It is by grace that may be of or through faith.

OMNIPRESENCE.—This follows from the last two attributes, omniscience and omnipotence, the power of knowing and acting everywhere ; God present, in His power and knowledge, everywhere. The definition has been suggested, " the presence of all things to God." This, while intended to keep clear of materialistic conceptions, at the same time does not fully express the idea intended—that of the essential as well as effective presence of God in all things and in all places. In one aspect of His being God is transcendent ; transcends the universe of His creatures as He does their capacity of comprehension ; the Holy One, separate and distinct from all finite beings and things. In another, He is immanent—distinct from and present in every movement and to every creature in His dominions. While there has been a tendency to run this truth into pantheism, so as to identify God and the world, yet this is not its necessity. It is the distinctness of existence, and yet, in that distinctness, the ever-abiding and everywhere pervading presence of that Spirit, in its perfection of knowing and of acting. Special manifestations of that presence may be made, and are scripturally described ; but every such special manifestation is only the fuller revelation of the ever-present and abiding reality. "Do not I fill heaven and earth ? saith Jehovah" (Jer. 23 : 24). " Our God is in the heavens" (Ps. 115 : 3). " He dwelleth not in temples made with hands" (Acts 17 : 24 ; see also Isa. 66 : 1 ; John 14 : 23 ; 1 Kings 8 : 27).

The sacramental issue of controversy, it is to be remembered, is not as to the presence of our Lord's Deity, but that of His body, His bodily humanity. He, as God, is present in the sacrament, as He is everywhere. He, as God Man, is at the right hand of the Father. Body, an outlined object, in becoming ubiquitous gets away from that which is the essential attribute of body, becomes omnipresent, is deified.

MORAL ATTRIBUTES.—The transition, here, from those already indicated, will be easily recognized. In the infinitude of being, of permanence, of power, of knowledge, and of presence, there is no necessary implication of moral relations or issues. Unconsciously, indeed, we carry with us in our idea of these attributes that of their moral exercise ; and it may be said that in the truth of infinite perfection, as personality, they are included. At the same time, they may and should be distinguished—the Divine attributes which are implied in the idea of moral and spiritual perfection. They are sometimes spoken of as attributes of the Divine will—as its forms of exertion and outworking, in contrast to those of simple power or intelligence ; as expressions, in such exercise, of the Divine will and character.

Without making distinct and separate sections in the examination of these, we may briefly notice their nature and connection. They are those of holiness, truth, justice, wisdom, and love or goodness.

The first of these—holiness—really including some of the others in its significance, is that of moral and spiritual excellence. This idea of holiness, as related to finite creatures, is that of consecration, separateness from everything impure or evil, separation, consecration to that which is excellent, to Him who is excellent, the Holy One. He, the Holy One, is infinitely separated from and against all evil and imperfection. He is thus set apart from, consecrated above all imperfect beings and things, in the excellence of His spiritual perfection. This word holy is often thought of only in its negative aspect—that of freedom from its opposite. Its positive thus fails of recognition. Both need to be kept in view. Holy (Saxon, *halig, hal*), hale, healthy, soundness, wholeness, is the significance of the word physically, as to the bodily organism. Bodily haleness, healthiness, wholeness, holiness of organic life, is that, negatively, of freedom from all taint of organic disease and imperfection; positively that of vigorous and active capacity. So, too, with that which is spiritual. As bringing out this truth of holiness in its positive aspect, it is sometimes used in Scripture as the equivalent of the Divine majesty (Isa. 6:3), as in the Apocalypse, the whiteness, not only absence of all tarnish and impurity, but the shining white resplendence of the Divine glory and majesty. See Matt. 17:2; Mark 9:3; Rev. 1:14, where it is not only purity, innocence, but glorious excellence.

Old Testament revelation brings out this truth of the Divine character: "I, the Lord thy God, am holy" (Lev.

19 : 2). He was thus holy in His purity and separateness from all the pollutions and abominations of heathen worship, and their impure objects of worship, in His supreme deity; above them and in His holiness opposed to them, as the only proper object of reverence and imitation. "Be ye holy" is the accordant precept of the New Testament, quoted from the Old Testament. "For I am holy" (1 Pet. 1 : 14, 16). "This is the will of God, your holiness" (1 Thess. 4 : 3). "Without holiness no man shall see the Lord" (Heb. 12 : 14). The finite holiness thus insisted upon finds its object in Him who is perfectly holy; free from all evil and possibility of evil, full of all moral and spiritual excellence.

But this supreme and perfect excellence, thus contemplated in its wholeness, negative and positive, has its forms of manifestation. One of these is that of truth. This we find scripturally as one of the Divine attributes. The truth of God, thus spoken of, has reference, first, to the truth and reality of His existence absolutely; as also relatively, in the way of opposition, to all other supposed or affirmed deities, and objects of worship or of reverence. He is the true God, the only God as opposed to all called or worshipped as gods. He is, moreover, the true God in that He is the God of truth. All His words are true. He is true in all His manifestations, in word and act, is what those manifestations profess and affirm. The truth of things is the exact correspondence of them with what they affirm or are represented to be. God is thus true in all His revelations of Himself; His declarations of promise and of warning ; His words as to the acts and character of His creatures. Herein is the ground of reliance to finite and human agents. "God is faithful" (1 Cor. 10 : 13), reliable, to be trusted, without reservation or hesitation, because He is true. "Thy word is truth" (John 17 : 17). "The judgments of Jehovah are true" (Ps. 19 : 9). "In faithfulness hast Thou afflicted me" (Ps. 119 : 75). "The word of the Lord is faithful, and everything He does is truth" (Ps. 33 : 4 ; 1 Cor. 1 : 9.)

Close akin to this is the attribute of righteousness or justice—the Divine perfection, working in and for righteousness as to all the movements of finite action, according to their real desert and character. This is sometimes described as holiness in action : moral and spiritual perfection brought into exercise ; opposing and chastening evil and wrong, sustaining, and helping, and rewarding the right. This quality in the character, and motives, and actions of moral beings is constantly implied in Scripture ; in particular cases, specifically asserted. They are right or wrong. As so, they are objects of Divine approval or condemnation ; of Divine administrative acts, in view of which the right will be vindicated, the wrong opposed, and finally be punished. It is a power not only working for righteousness, but in righteousness ; in that righteousness identified with the cause of the righteous, opposing and condemning its opposite. "God," says the psalmist, "will judge the world in righteousness." Such judgment is going on during the whole Divine administration; is finally perfected in the great day of final retribution.

This justice may thus be contemplated, first, in its legislative aspect; as expressing itself in laws and precepts, whether in the natural constitution of things, or as specifically revealed. It may be also looked at in its executive administration, enforcing those laws in one direction, warning against their violation in another; as judicial, rewarding the obedient and punishing the disobedient. The questions of natural and revealed laws, or of natural and positive rewards and penalties, may be more properly treated elsewhere. It is sufficient for our purpose that these features in the attribute of justice or righteousness be clearly recognized. God, as a God of holiness and righteousness, hating evil and loving right; in His law revealing His righteous will, as to the acts and motives of His creatures; in His dealings enforcing and sustaining those laws; in His judgments, rewarding and punishing. "The statutes of the Lord are right" (Ps. 19:8). "The perfect will of God" (Rom. 12:1). "Thou sittest in the throne judging right" (Ps. 9:4). "God judgeth the righteous, and is angry with the wicked" (Ps. 7:11). "Thy judgments are right" (Ps. 119:75).

The attribute of wisdom is not usually classified with the moral. As, however, distinct from knowledge, simple intelligence, it rather belongs here. Wisdom has been defined as "an exercise of the intellect into which the highest affections of the heart enter."

So, again, as knowing how to use knowledge; or the knowing good, to the attainment of good. As wisdom is thus intelligence plus the capacity of devising and attaining what is right and good, $\sigma o \varphi \iota \alpha$, חָכְמָה, so it is contrasted with craft, $\delta o \lambda o s$, עָרוּם, cunning, or even skill, in which the right and good may not be present, or in which may be sought their opposite. As related to knowledge, its meaning can only be brought out by some defining adjective; and that, as bringing out the moral element in its exercise. In the omniscience of God, for instance, we affirm His perfect knowledge of all things and of all beings; of his own perfections, as of the imperfections of His creatures. In His wisdom we affirm, further, the exercise of that knowledge, as in harmony with and dictated by His holiness, and truth, and righteousness, and love. In the harmonious co-operation of these attributes He is the only wise God, knowing and purposing good results; of blessing to all His subjects and creatures.

This implies ends contemplated, and means to be employed to their attainment. The final end, in creature action, as revealed in Scripture precept, is, that all be done to the glory of God. That which is thus presented as the ultimate end with the creature, is revealed as the end with the Creator. But God thus glorifies Himself in the creature by making that creature like Himself, in blessedness as well as in holiness. Doing the will of God, the creature glorifies God; in so doing becomes like Him, secures His approval, and the highest blessedness of which He is capable. God's ultimate end is to reveal Himself in His perfection of blessedness; in so doing to communicate Himself in that blessedness to His dependent creatures. The ultimate beatific vision of the redeemed is thus to "see Him as He is." As His glorious perfections are thus appreciated and appropriated, these His creatures are blessed and elevated.

As to the means of securing these ends, we may say that the best will always be taken. We are not capable of judging here. What may seem complicated, inadequate, or even inconsistent with the ends to be secured, may not only be the best, but really the simplest and shortest. Finite wisdom often needs a variety of means to secure a single end. Infinite, often through a single mean, may secure a variety of ends. In that effort and work every moment is filled up, and perfectly; and in the full result will be no waste of time, effort, or material. "The foolishness of God is wiser than men" (1 Cor. 1:25). "Jehovah by wisdom founded the earth" (Prov. 3:19). "O Lord, how manifold are Thy works; in wisdom hast Thou made them all" (Ps. 104:24). "O the depth of the riches, both of the wisdom and knowledge of God" (Rom. 11:33).

We thus reach what, in Scripture, is made the complement and completion of these attributes of moral perfection—that of love, goodness, benevolence. Two of these words express the Divine working of a certain character; the other the impulse to it, the Divine love. "God is love." He is holy, and true, and righteous, and wise; and He is loving. In the exercise of these others and of all His attributes He is not indifferent as to the interests and welfare of those to whom, in such working, they have regard. As His creatures, called by Him into existence, reflecting to some degree His perfections, they are objects of His love. This love goes out in goodness, in blessing to the creature to the extent of his capacity of reception. Question has been raised, and the effort made, to resolve all the moral attributes into this one of love, benevolence; to represent them as different forms of its operation. The difficulty, however, to this is that the ideas of these other attributes are simple, not resolvable into others. The words describing them refer to distinct characteristics, and are thus employed in Scripture. In such usage, too, we see that there is a guard against the error of making Divine love that of mere sentimentalism; that which is indiscriminate, and without reference to character. And yet, while we cannot resolve these attributes into love, we must remember it as in them all, as in them effectively operative. The tendency of Christian theology, at one period, was to emphasize another of these atttributes, that of justice, to the losing sight of others; at another, that of almighty power. The present tendency is to forget these in the affirmation of love. The problem is to take account of all; and, in the fulness and emphasis of the Divine revelation of love, to find its place; its propulsion, so to speak, in every Divine act, whether of power, righteousness, or wisdom. " God is love" is one of the last utterances as to His character and action. "The love of God, in Jesus Christ our Lord," the ground of human confidence and consolation. As we thus find holiness, the entireness of the Divine moral excellence, so we find love, the element pervading them all, and bringing blessing in their operation. It is of the essence of love to seek to bless its object. In that seeking there will be no sacrifice of any other perfection, but rather its enforcement and highest illustration.

See Knapp, Dwight, and Hodge, and especially Dr. Fairchild s "Elements of Theology," for this and the section following.

CHAPTER IX.

THE DOCTRINE OF TRINITY.

In what sense a mystery.—Threefoldness in unity.—Natural analogies.—Ground of reception, and position in New Testament teaching.—How far to be found in Old Testament.—Two general classes of passages in New Testament.—What to be established as to the Son and Blessed Spirit.—Passages in which these truths are exhibited.—Economy of the Divine Revelation, as to this doctrine.

In the unity of God, the infinitude of the Divine perfection, we have mystery, not in the sense of the undiscoverable, but in that of the incomprehensible. The one God, "God over all, blessed forever," transcending all human, all finite capacity of comprehension—a necessity of human thought, and yet, to human thought, the great mystery.

In the Trinity, the Triunity, the threefoldness in unity, or unity in threefoldness of God, revealed in the New Testament, it may be said that there is mystery in both of these senses—the undiscoverable and the incomprehensible. Its difficulty, however, is not so much its incomprehensibility, in either one or both of these senses, as in its supposed or apparent contradiction; the three in one or the one in three. Understanding it to mean that God is one and three, in all respects exactly alike and the same, there would be such contradiction. There is no necessity for any such statement. There are many forms of finite threefoldness perfectly consistent with unity. If so with the finite, much more with the infinite. We find that, in the affirmation of this threefoldness, there are distinctions indicating differences; the persons, related to each other in the Divine unity, are severally related to men in the work of redemption. There is thus indicated one God, one Divine nature. In this Divine nature are the distinctions of Father, Son, and Holy Ghost; and these equally and in common have the nature and perfections of Supreme Deity. How thus in all respects three and one, Scripture does not say. Its object, rather, is to exhibit this truth in its connection with human redemption; in its adaptation to human necessity.

As to the difficulties of threefoldness in unity, effort has been made, in the way of analogy, to remove them. The threefoldness, in the unity of human nature, of body, soul, and spirit; that, again, in the spiritual nature of man, of intelligence, sensibility and will; those, again, of unity, in manifoldness of relations, as son, father, and brother; or, further, again, of that one human being in varied manifestations—all these may help to remove the difficulties. As are all human analogies, these are in the sphere of the finite, and touch, perhaps, at only one point. The essential question is: Have we this truth clearly exhibited in the teaching of Christ and His apostles? What is its substance and place in that teaching; its practical application? We may, as we suppose, see reasons for it prior to all Scripture teaching. We may see such reasons for it, after it has been clearly taught. But the real question is that already stated: Has God spoken in this matter? What is His meaning?

In seeking the reply to this, we first notice the place of this doctrine in the Christian system. It is primary, fundamental. The apostles were sent out to baptize men into a profession of it, as heartily accepted. As men thus knew Father, Son, and Holy Ghost, they came savingly in contact with the great redemptive features of Christianity. It may be said that this doctrine constitutes the spinal column of the Christian system. It forms the main substance of the early creeds. Those creeds, indeed, are only enlargements of the early baptismal formula of Matt. 28 : 19, and are introductory to all the doctrinal contents of the New Testament. We thus look at this New Testament teaching.

The question as to the teaching of the Old Testament on this doctrine has been differently answered. Some of its declarations, read in the light of the New Testament, are strikingly significant. It must be said that, if contained in these passages, the doctrine was not recognized by Old Testament readers. The logos of Alexandrian Judaism hovers between a personified attribute and a personality. The same may be said of the Memra Jehovah of the Rabbinic theology. The angel Jehovah, in one part of the narrative distinguished from Jehovah, and in another identified with

Him, has its bearing in the same direction. So, too, passages speaking of the Spirit of God in the Old Testament, the passage standing by itself may mean either an attribute or a personality. The specific classes of passages usually quoted on this topic are fourfold.

(*a*) Those in which plurality of names and actions is affirmed. "Elohim said"—singular verb—"let us"—plural—"make man." Elohim said, "Let *us* go down" (Gen. 11 : 7). Jehovah said, "Who will go for us?" (Isa. 6 : 8).

(*b*) Where the names are separated and distinguished. "Jehovah rained fire and brimstone from Jehovah" (Gen. 19 : 24). "O our God, hear our prayer, for the Lord's sake" (Dan. 9 : 17). "Jehovah said to my Lord" (Ps. 110 : 1).

(*c*) The names of Son and Spirit in the Old Testament. "And now Jehovah and His Spirit hath sent me" (Isa. 48 : 16). "The heavens were made by the word of the Lord, and the host of them by the breath of His mouth" (Ps. 33 : 6).

(*d*) Threefoldness of expression. "Jehovah bless thee," etc. (Num. 6 : 24). "Holy, holy, holy" (Isa. 6 : 3).

Any one of these passages or classes, taken by itself, might not have importance as proof. All taken together constitute a problem, of which the New Testament doctrine of the Trinity is the satisfactory solution. Read in the light of that New Testament revelation, many of those passages are full of profound significance.

Passing on to the New Testament, we find a twofold classification of passages: those of a collective and those of an individual character. In the first, the persons are mentioned together. In the second, they are mentioned singly. To the former we, therefore, first give attention. These are the apostolic commission, Matt. 3:16, 17; 28:19, 20; 1 Pet. 1:2; John 14:26; 2 Cor. 13:14; Eph. 2:18; Rev. 1:4, 5.

As a summary of the contents of these, we find: First, association of three names or subjects, one of whom is undoubtedly personal deity. Second, personality is explicitly affirmed of the second, and necessarily implied in what is said of the third. Third, the order of mention is not invariable; the second sometimes first, the third, second or first (2 Cor. 13:14; 1 Pet. 1:1, 2; Rev. 1:4, 5; Eph. 2:1, 8). Fourth, such collocation, as also the change of the order and the common fact of personality, suggest equality.

In passing from these to the second class of passages, those in which mention is made of Father, Son, and Holy Ghost separately, the two points needing to be established are, first, their personality, then their deity. As to the Father and the Son, there is no doubt as to the personality. This needs especially to be proved of the Holy Spirit. So, again, there is no question as to the Deity of the Father. Recognizing the twofold scriptural application of the term Father, sometimes as the Divine Being or nature, and then, more specifically, in His relation to the second person, the Son, we pass on to the examination of the passages bearing upon the two points thus mentioned: the Deity of the Son, the personality and deity of the Holy Ghost.

First, then, as to the Deity of the Son. This is found in passages which give Him Divine names; which affirm of Him Divine attributes and works; which involve expressions of adoration and worship. A Being who is to be called God, who has the perfections of God, and is to be worshipped as God, is to be regarded as God, as a Divine being.

As to the first, Divine names (John 1:1), "The Word was God." "I and My Father are one" (John 10:28, 30). "My Lord and My God" (John 20:28). "Equal with God" (Phil. 2:6). Examine Rom. 9:5 and Titus 1:4; 2:13.

And as Divine names are thus applied to the Son, so we find also Divine attributes and works. Eternity, in John 17:5; 8:58: "The glory which I had with Thee before the world was." "Before Abraham was, I am." Creative power, in John 1:2; Col. 1:15, 17; Phil. 3:21; Heb. 1:3; John 5:17–20. "All things were made by Him." "By Him were all things made in heaven and in earth." "Upholding all things by the word of His power." "He is able to subdue all things unto Himself." "No one knoweth the Father but the Son" (Matt. 11:27).

And these Divine names, and attributes, and works ascribed to Him are accompanied by expressions of reverence and acts of worship, as to a Divine being. "Show, Lord, whom Thou hast chosen" (Acts 1:24).

"Lord Jesus, receive my spirit" (Acts 7 : 59, 60). "At or in the name of Jesus every knee should bow" (Phil. 2 : 10). "I besought the Lord thrice" (2 Cor. 12 : 8). "All men should honor the Son even as they honor the Father" (John 5 : 23).

In the proof of the Deity of the blessed Spirit, the Holy Ghost, that of His personality first claims attention—the fact that in speaking of the Spirit of God the Scriptures do not mean merely a power, or attribute, or such attribute personified, but a Divine person, possessed of all the Divine attributes. We look, therefore, first at the language as to this point, and then, further, as to Divine nature and perfection.

One of the first of these may be seen in the language of our Lord, in John 14 and 16, as to the Paraclete or Helper, who, on His departure, would take His place. This language describes not a power, but a person. "He would lead them into all truth." "He would teach them;" "would call all things to their remembrance" of His previous teaching; "would convict the world of sin;" "would show them things to come;" would reveal the real and full significance of Christ's work and person. He is thus described by the masculine $εκεινος$, not it, but He. So, further, in 1 Cor. 12 : 4–11, He imparts $χαρισματα$, distinct from Himself. He is distinguished from $κυριος$ and from $θεος$, and imparts His gifts autocratically, $καθως βουλεται$, "as He will."

And this personality, thus described, is in these passages, as in others, also spoken of as exercising Divine powers. In 1 Cor. 2 : 10 He reveals truth, searches the depth of infinitude, "the deep things of God;" in Acts 13 : 2-4 orders the separation of Paul and Barnabas. These show that, in the collective passages, as Matt. 28 and 2 Cor. 12 : 13, personality is involved. This person thus exercises the attributes of omniscience, of omnipotence, of omnipresence, of wisdom.

As to Divine worship, we find, in Rom. 9 : 1, the Holy Spirit is invoked by the apostle as present to know the truth of his assertion ; and in Matt. 12 : 31, "blasphemy against the Holy Ghost" is spoken of as an offence of the deepest malignity.

Again, as to Divine names, we find, in Acts 5 : 3, 4, that lying against the Holy Ghost is spoken of as lying against God. The names are interchanged. If it be said that lying against Peter, as appointed of God, would have been lying against God, the reply is, that in the one case the creaturely character of the mediate agent would be undoubted, in the other it is not. Standing by itself, this text might not be sufficient as full proof of Deity of the blessed spirit. That proof is seen as it is taken with others.

In glancing over these passages, as to the Deity of the second and third persons of the adorable Trinity, there is exhibited a specialty, and amplification, and profuseness as to the second which is not found with the third. The explanation seems to be twofold. First, the difficulty of plurality in unity is encountered in the issue of our Lord's Deity ; after this there was less need of such variety of statement and amplification. Second, the idea of divineness, power, knowledge, wisdom was already familiar, and associated with the idea of the Spirit of God. The development of doctrine really needed was the truth of His personality. When this became clear, the doctrine assumed its full proportions. Old passages of the law and the prophets were read with a new meaning. Just as the old meanings of Son of God, angels, good men, magistrates, or a being called by creative act into existence, came to include all these meanings, and something divinely more, so to these old meanings of the Spirit of God, Divine power, or knowledge, or wisdom, or these personified, was added that of the personal Holy Ghost, the Lord and Giver of life, with the Father and the Son to be worshipped and glorified.

There is a profound significance in the suggestion of Archbishop Whately as to the Divine rationale, so to speak, of the lateness of the clear and distinct revelation of this doctrine of the Trinity: that of its practical application and importance. Prior to the actual manifestation of the second Person in the work of human redemption, and that of the blessed Spirit in its living application, the doctrine of the Trinity, even if intelligible, would have been largely speculative. As it is, it is seen to touch every part, and to meet every necessity of human nature. It is thus a doctrine not to speculate about, but to appropriate and live upon: God, a loving Father, in the infinite self-sacrifice and the gift of his well-beloved Son; God, a Divine-Human Brother, knowing, feeling with, and able to help His human brethren ; God, an ever-present Spirit in life, and in effect enlightening, sustaining, and consoling in all human trial and experience, making Divine truth living and energetic in human minds and hearts ; God, Father, Son, and Holy Ghost, thus the God of human nature, in the fulness of whose revelation all the wants and aspirations of this nature are met and satisfied.

CHAPTER X.

CREATION AND ORIGIN OF THE WORLD.

The idea of creation.—Different from that of mere arrangement.—How related to theories of Evolution.—Divine Preservation, Providence, and Government.

The truth of the Divine Trinity, of the Divine Unity in its threefoldness of manifestation and working, has more special reference to the world of men—moral and spiritual beings in spiritual relations to God and to each other. God the Father, God the Son, and God the Holy Ghost are alike spoken of in creation. So, too, they all co-operate in redemption; but each one in His special mode. God the Father loves the world, and, in the self-sacrifice of love, sends His well-beloved Son for its deliverance. God the Son, in like love and self-sacrifice, comes and takes upon Him human nature, working and suffering for its benefit. God the Holy Ghost reveals and makes these truths savingly effectual. The Trinity is thus the doctrine of God as related to a world of moral and spiritual beings; is specially adapted to the necessities of these beings as fallen and sinful.

The truth of the Divine Unity, while in most important respects related to man, is more predominantly so in Scripture to the world of creation, as called into existence, sustained and regulated. In the question, therefore, of the origin and creation of the world, including our own system, or any of which we have knowledge, we contemplate the Divine Unity. "God," said the apostle to his Athenian hearers, "that made the world and all things therein." This has its positive meaning. It has in view opposing affirmations; and it is connected with practical inferences of the highest practical importance. To some of these we give examination.

Manifestly, in this particular case, it was intended to assert the unity of the Creator of the world against the multitude of deities worshipped by his hearers. This is its frequent implication in the Old and New Testament. "To us there is but one God." "He made the world, and all that is therein." The claims of all others, therefore, are empty and false. "In the beginning God created the heaven and the earth;" not only our earth or planet, but whatever else is included in the heavens. "Thou, Lord," said the psalmist, "in the beginning hast laid the foundations of the earth, and the heavens are the work of Thy hands" (Ps. 102 : 25). "He that created the heavens and stretched them out" (Isa. 42 : 5). "The heaven, even the heaven of heavens, is the Lord's" (Ps. 115 : 16). "Hath not My hand made all things?" (Acts 7 : 50.) "Of Him, and through Him, and to Him are all things" (Rom. 11 : 36). The origin of the world, of the heaven and the earth, as they now are in these passages, is clearly affirmed, as in the Divine will and working.

But the issue is made of the difference between creation—that which calls things into existence, not forming and arranging existing material, but calling the material itself into existence; creation in the strict sense of the word. The effort has been to find in these passages only the ordering and arrangement of pre-existing material—the transformation of chaos into cosmos. "*Ex nihilo, nihil fit*" was the maxim of heathen philosophy, as it is sometimes now of naturalistic unbelief. But infinitude, the infinitude of the Divine perfection, is not *nihil*. In His resources all such difficulties are imaginary. The matter, the atoms, the vortices, or whatever their name, elementary to the coming cosmos, must be created, or it must originate itself. Things do not come just dry so. They must exist uncaused, or they must find a cause adequate to their origination. Such adequate Cause is Infinite Perfection—God! Agnosticism, while affirming ignorance as to the character and actions of such sufficient Cause, finds it a necessity to world existence. The only originating efficient of cause of which we have knowledge is that of mind and will, the originative power of moral and spiritual beings. Human thought is thus forced to the conclusion of inspired truth. "God," not merely the Framer or Disposer, but the "Creator of the heavens and the earth."

As to the language of Scripture, it falls in with this idea of creation. "There are," says Dean Smith, "three words employed in the Old Testament in reference to the production of the world—בָּרָא, He created; יָצַר, He formed; and עָשָׂה, He made—the first term being appropriated exclusively to God alone, who is alone called Creator. Creation, therefore, according to the Hebrew, is a Divine act; though, according to its etymology, it does not necessarily imply a creation out of nothing, it does signify the Divine production of something new, something that did not exist before. "It denotes," says Delitzsch, "a Divine and miraculous production, having its commencement in time." The expression, "God said, let it be, and it was," is, perhaps, the most striking of all these forms. As the similar one elsewhere, "He spake, and it was done."

Nor are these statements confined to the simple fact of originating material. One form of speculation denies this truth of Divine origination. Another, admitting this, denies its continued operation. The inspired record affirms both. It goes on and exhibits the Creator as arranging and ordering the material, through the ages, to the production of the present condition of things; by which the world was organized and brought into condition for animal and human habitation. בָּרָא, as we have seen, is used of the first, "God created." And then, following, in the other words and forms of expression, are described His continued action and supervision. The operation of Divine law, material, chemical, vegetable, and organic forces, is not, by the Divine will, excluded. At the same time, the operation of these does not and cannot exclude the presence and agency of Him who called them into existence—originating not only the material, but its laws and forces. If this be called evolution, there is no difficulty with it, if it be recognized as the working out of the previous involution of the Divine purpose, as the accompanying Divine agency, controlling it to His designed result. His hand is in and over the evolution, as is His mind, His purpose in the involution. God is present and operative in both of these respects all through the whole chapter of Genesis, as He is in the first verse. In the different stages He is present. He speaks, and results follow; He directs as to processes, and those processes are accomplished; He approves them as "good," as "very good," as adequate to His intended purposes. The process, too, it may be said, is in what is now seen to be the natural order of forces and operations.* It begins with matter, with its principles of gravity and affinity; it rises from this to the vegetable world, with its principle of vitality; it rises from this to the animal world, with its principles of sensation and instinct. And it rises from this to man, in his world, and with his powers of rational and moral reflection and action. Each step rests upon, takes in the former, and is something additional. At every such step comes in the Divine Creator, and in each, calling out, for the new stage, its laws and principles of existence. Of course Moses, or whoever wrote this chapter, knew nothing of this scientific order; but

* See Hopkins's Outline Man.

somehow or other, he has described it. "The heavens and the earth, and the generations of them," were thus, in Divine creative power, counsel, and agency; in His arrangement and supervision of their varied forms and modes of existence and operation. This conclusion, thus, first against polytheism, is no less against materialism; involves the supreme ownership of Jehovah, the God of Israel, as He is of the whole earth.

PRESERVATION, PROVIDENCE, GOVERNMENT.—Following naturally upon the truth of Divine creation is that of preservation—the continuance of beings and things, with their manifold forms and modes of existence and operation. All beings, all things, in the light of Scripture, as in that of rational conclusion, are to God in the relation of absolute dependence. They are thus dependent upon Him, first, for existence; still further, for its continuance; still further for their powers of action and enjoyment; for the capacity of exercising those powers; for the objects to which they are related. Divine preservation has been called a continued creation. Distinction, however, is properly made between the two—the calling into existence and the perpetuation of such existence. The distinction of immediate and mediate creation would better describe it. In both, however, is the common truth of the Divine presence and effective working; and, in the last, as clearly revealed, is there provision against the tendency of human thought to stop at the existing forces and laws of the natural work, as exhaustive of all the agencies to its preservation and perpetuation. Pascal said of Descartes, that his only use for God, in the world, was to give it a fillip, in the way of a start, after it was made, and leave it to its own laws and forces. This is the view of the old English deism, communicated by them to the Germans, and called rationalism, more properly naturalism, and has come back again into English thought, as materialistic evolution; in this, its last form, getting rid even of Descartes' Divine Creator, as of the fillip, starting creation on its progress. The properly descriptive name for this, in all its forms, as already intimated, is naturalism. Sometimes it is materialistic; sometimes, as including all natural powers and agencies, those of mind as of matter; but finding explanation of all the phenomena of the world, for its continued preservation, as for all its forms of existence of action, in the operation of these natural agencies. Miracle, the supernatural, the manifestation and working in nature of the Author of nature, is thus excluded, is ruled out as impossible.

Over against this, is the truth of the Divine presence and agency, in the continuance of the world, as in its creation. Just as in the creative days God was thus present and operative in the successive stages, from matter up to man, and in the operation of the laws then called forth, so is He now, ever has been, and will be in the world's continuance. "The Lord is good to all, and His tender mercy is over all His works." "Thou openest Thy hand, and satisfiest the desire of every living thing" (Ps. 145 : 9, 15). So also Ps. 147. "Thine hands have made me and fashioned me" (Job

10 : 8). "In Him we live, and move, and are" (Acts 17 : 28). "Not one of them forgotten before God" (Luke 12 : 6). "Your heavenly Father feedeth them" (Matt. 6 : 26). Manifestly there is here the implication as the assertion of Divine presence and agency to the world's continuance and preservation. In His ordinances, whether of heaven or of earth, and giving them effectiveness, He, the God of preservation as of creation, is present and operative.

Closely connected with this truth of Divine preservation are those of providence and government. The first has more special reference to a present arrangement and control of created things and beings from moment to moment as they move on ; the latter in the present also, but controlling and overruling for the future. How such providential agency is exercised, in what manner it extends to the minutest as to the greatest matters ; how it adjusts itself to and uses natural laws and forces ; in what manner it uses, or baffles, or overrules human agency without at all infringing upon human freedom and accountability, we are not told ; would not, perhaps, if told, be able to comprehend. But the truth itself is clearly revealed and distinctly emphasized. "He doeth His will in the armies of heaven, and among the inhabitants of the earth" (Dan. 4 : 35). "He maketh all things work together for good to them that love Him" (Rom. 8 : 28). "Herod, and Pontius Pilate, and the Jewish rulers are described as working out their own counsels. And yet, while thus working freely for their own ends, without intending or knowing, they accomplish the Divine purpose. The reign of law, material, physical, and rational, is thus secured. At the same time, in the providential Divine administration, it does not exclude the personal presence and agency of its Divine Author and Giver. In His providence these laws, in their operation, are made consistent with His special designs and purposes. " In Him we live, and move, and are." He reveals Himself as an ever-present help in every time of trouble. Prayer, as dictated by the exigencies of the present necessity, which, to be answered, demands the exercise of present Divine power, must, in faith, be made to Him. Creatures, in such prayer, are to go to Him as children to a Father in every exigency. And they have the assurance, not only of the Father's heart to sympathize, but that the Father's hand, all-sufficient for help, will be put forth to their benefit. To Him in His providence all things, small and great alike, as needed, are possible. The revelation of Him in the microscope is no less wonderful than of that in the telescope. Details do not exclude general principles; and general principles do not exclude details. (See Ps. 107; 113; Matt. 7; Luke 12.) It may, indeed, be said that this is the scriptural assumption everywhere—God at hand, providing and present to all the wants and earnest petitions of His creatures.

And these two truths, Divine preservation and providence, lead naturally to, if they do not imply, Divine government. In this are the ideas of purpose, plan, ends to be attained, an ultimate end to which subordinates have reference. In the counsel of Divine perfection, that end cannot be anything imperfect and limited. "Jehovah hath made all things for Himself." That ultimate end is the manifestation of Himself in His perfections as in His blessedness to His creatures, thus imparting to them in Himself the highest good of which they are capable. As they "see Him they become like Him."

But, to this ultimate end, there are intermediates exhibited in the Divine administration; sometimes in the Church, sometimes in the world. They are brought to view in the history of the race in the various stages of human experience. They are more conspicuously exhibited in His revealed dispensations, His dealings with His servants and ancient people, His preparations in these for the final manifestation of His purposes of blessing and salvation. So, too, in the affairs of this world, as in Scripture, He governs against evil and wrong and on the side of righteousness. The great purpose running through all these is the establishment of a kingdom of righteousness. And the assurance is given that this shall eventually become the controlling and pervading power in humanity. "All things are to come to a head in Christ." "God is to be all in all." Creation begins with God, calling all things into being. God preserves and guides. God rules and controls. God not only thus rules, but He shall be openly acknowledged and lovingly obeyed as Ruler. God's kingdom in a redeemed and glorified world is the blessed termination—the end which has no ending.

The relation of these truths to the fact of the existence of evil will come up in connection with the subject of sin. For the present we may briefly summarize the theories under which these truths have been construed.

The first has already been intimated: God creating and imposing forces and laws upon the world and leaving it to their operation.

The second is the extreme of this, and rather loses sight of natural laws and forces in the Divine immanence, acting directly in all movements and operations. To some degree, too, this Divine immanence gets away from the idea of the Divine personality, or fails to give it due position. With some it seems to be the old truth of the omnipresence of power, as of love and knowledge, of a Divine personality. In others it seems to identify the immanent power with that in which it is working, and thus to run into pantheistic conceptions. To say the least, the modes of expression are not at all satisfactory. God is in the world immanent; but also, distinct from the world, He is transcendent.

The last is that which finds the Divine Creator, and Preserver, and Provider, and Governor, as also His laws. At the same time, while He has an ordinary mode of operation as the basis of action and calculation to finite creatures, yet He Himself is not tied to it. For reasons sufficient, effects may be contemplated and extraordinary means used to their accomplishment—in other words, miracles. Miracle is not necessarily contradictory to natural law, is not suspension of such law. It is a higher power coming in, affecting, and modifying laws and forces to a new result. He who knows all, who sustains all, and is able to control all, can do this without confusion.

Duke of Argyle's "Reign of Law" and "Unity of Nature."
Harris's "Self-Revelation of God."
McCosh's "Divine Government."
Cudworth's "System of the Universe."
Dawson's "Origin of the World."

CHAPTER XI.

THE DOCTRINE OF MAN.

His original condition.—Divine image, its Scriptural meanings.—Unity of the race.—Possibilities of primeval acquisition.—The first act of transgression and fall.

MAN IN HIS PRIMEVAL CONDITION.—"God," said Koheleth, "hath made everything beautiful in its time." "God said," is the record of Genesis, "let us make man in our own image, after our likeness, and let them have dominion." The world, in its Divine creation and order of preservation, providence, and overruling control, is thus contemplated in subordination to the dominion of man. Man, really in God's image, will rule in accordance with God's will and purposes, and this His rule will be a blessing to all creation. So far as he is in that image, morally and spiritually, will this result be secured. The scriptural account of man follows that of his creation; and this in its relation to all that follows. Some of the particulars of that account claim attention.

First, then, as to the significance of this expression, the "image and likeness of God." The first of these words, צלם, describes the outline of an object as cast by its shadow; the other, דמ, that of resemblance in general. The former the image of God, that most frequently used, seems intended to express the idea of what is peculiar to humanity as distinct from or contrasted with the lower orders of creation. Sometimes it is as in its Divine ideal as before the fall; sometimes only in its actual human natural, and after that event; but always as thus with the Divine impress of essential human nature. In the first two chapters of Genesis, for instance, the predominant idea of the Divine image, as resemblance, seems to be that of Divine dominion; as God over all, so man under Him in his dominion of the lower creation. This, too, is the idea of the New Testament in one place (1 Cor. 11 : 7), where man, as the image of God, is over the woman. In Gen. 9 : 6, however, where the prohibition against murder is based upon the fact of this Divine image in the victim; and in James 3 : 9, where the cursing of men, in this Divine image, is reprobated, it seems to be rather the essential fact of humanity that is indicated, and without specific reference either to dominion or character; while in Col. 3 : 10, where the regenerate man is spoken of "as renewed in knowledge after the image of Him that created Him;" and in Eph. 4 : 23, 24, when such an one is spoken of "as renewed in the spirit of his mind; as putting on the new man, which after God is created in righteousness and true holiness," the idea manifestly is that of the Divine image of moral and spiritual resemblance. These three classes of passages bring before us, it may be said, the three stages and forms of human experience to which this expression is applicable: The image of God to man in his innocence, as he was created, and before he sinned. The image of God in his humanity, marred and defaced by sin, but not hopelessly obliterated and destroyed. The image of God, in his spiritual restoration and transformation in Christ, and through the power of His renewing Spirit; this latter the earnest and prophecy of the Divine image in humanity in its heavenly excellence, glorified with Christ in His heavenly exaltation.

Humanity thus spoken of, as in the Divine image, in its totality, is also thus implied as to its particulars—in its bodily, its vitalized and spiritual characteristics. Man's body, like that of other creatures, certainly after the fall, is subject to the law of change and dissolution. Evidently had there been no such fall, the implication was that of continued bodily existence, but nothing of its particulars; the transition from the natural to the spiritual body, not by death, but in some other way. Besides the body, is mention made of the soul, נפש, as an organific principle, sometimes very nearly the equivalent of life, but of a life not necessarily destroyed by bodily death. Sometimes, again, soul is very nearly, if not quite, the equivalent of spirit, רוח, the spiritual being in personality. And then, further, the word spirit describes this last idea of personality, and more specifically. Soul and spirit seem to be interchanged in the Old Testament poetic parallelism, as they are sometimes in the New Testament. If there be any difference in such cases, it is that soul, as in modern psychology, indicates connection with organism, spirit as dwelling in the body. Spirit itself is not contemplated as necessarily in such relation. In 1 Thess. 5 : 23 the three, "body, soul, and spirit," are spoken of together as the objects of the whole sanctification prayed for by the apostle. In Heb. 4 : 12 "soul and spirit" are spoken of in connection with the thoughts and intents of the heart, and these as related to bodily organism. Body and spirit are thus clearly distinguished. Soul is connected ordinarily with body, as also with spirit. In this idea of spirit, spiritual personality is usually the implication of continued existence; and the glorified body and sanctified soul and spirit are contemplated as the final condition of the redeemed race—every part of human nature delivered from the effects of evil and sin—in Christ positively exalted and glorified.

Implied in these particulars has been that of the unity of the race—the fact of its unity of origin as contrasted with the various characteristics of different peoples and nations at the present time. This, at one time a sharply contested point of dispute, has lost much of its interest. In the later issue of the derivation of man from a lower order of organic being, that of his unity has been accepted on both sides. This is manifestly the implication of Scripture. Men are spoken of as having a common nature, as of a common origin. "God," says the apostle, "hath made of one blood all nations of men to dwell on the face of the earth." Blood is, perhaps, not critically correct; but nature, or something to that effect, needs to be supplied. The race fell in one man; by one man is redeemed. Its unity is the base of all such representations.

Just here a deeply interesting question presents itself, one a subject of much discussion and speculation—that of man's possibilities of knowledge and of acquisition, as a being thus called into existence; and with this that of the possibility of a primitive revelation. Whether created or evolved from a lower organism, this question presents itself. The rational and moral being, however he came, when he came, encountered this problem. How, and how far, as such being, can he know and be receptive of knowledge? Regarding him as created, we may briefly examine this question. How, for instance, with such a being as to language? The reply to this will be substantially the same as to other acquisitions.

Here mere natural analogies fail. And the difficulties urged from such analogies ignore the fact that a created man, as divinely called into existence, is not a natural, but a supernatural phenomenon. So, too, with a rational nature communicated to one of the higher forms of brute existence.* Such a man would not be an infant as to his digestive, his muscular, or his nervous system. He would not be so in his intellectual, his emotional, his volitional nature. Just as such a one would move, and walk, and take food, and take cognizance of surrounding objects, so would

---

* Nature, as from *nascor natus*, that which in some manner is born, or from φυσις ϕυω, that which grows or has grown, does not describe what is here spoken of.

he make signs, and give sounds, expressive of ideas, especially as not alone, but, as like the created man, with a companion—this companion, being no less necessary to the evolved man, if his race is to be perpetuated. The beginnings would, of course, be imperfect; but the progress would be rapid. In such case there would be a power and rapidity of movement, in all lines of capacity and acquisition, of which we have no analogous instances. Given the fact of such a being, or two such beings, in daily association; and as would be the necessity, so would be the development of capacity, both of thought, and its expression in word or in action. All that we can say with certainty is, that as the exigency came, so the sign or the sound needing to constitute expression would come along with it. Language, as thus the expression and outcome of thought, would increase and enlarge its means of expression.

Aiding this would be any specific Divine communications of which he might be in the reception. How exactly they were made, how "Elohim said," we are not specifically told. God is described as speaking, as making Himself intelligible to man; and man, it is implied, understood the Divine communication. The extreme of naturalism, which would construe the first man as a helpless infant, is as absurd as that of some of the old theologians, who found him in full possession of all the acquisitions of the subsequent race. Between these is the position described in Genesis: a being capable of acquiring knowledge, and becoming more intelligent, as intelligence was needed; of thus coming into communication with the world around, as with his Maker; and, in that knowledge, capable of moral accountability—of moral excellence or its failure. Thus we find him in Genesis, with language, the religious institution of the Sabbath, the moral and social of the marriage relation, bodily employment, in keeping the garden, as a condition of healthful physical existence. And thus far, in the language of his Divine Creator, very good.

THE FIRST TRANSGRESSION AND FALL.—The transition from the last topic is natural: that of man in Eden, to the first transgression and its effects. This last has its difficulties: first, as to interpretation; second, as to its effects upon the man himself, and through him upon his posterity. Just here we look at the first, its interpretation.

These are threefold: the allegorical, the mythical, and the literal. The difficulty with the first two is the variety of meanings extracted by them from the narrative, and their conflicting character. That which proves everything proves nothing. The difficulty with the literal is mainly with the serpent, and the character of the trees and their fruit. These, however, are not insuperable. It is to be said, moreover, that the human part, the moral and spiritual transactions, whether clothed in figure or not, are clear and unmistakable as to their meaning—to all intents and purposes may be treated as literalities. The human agents were placed upon trial; they were tempted, disobeyed, and fell; they were subjected to penalty.

The literalities of that penalty are unquestionable. Some of these we examine.*

One of these is the fact which gives significance to the whole: that of trial, test of obedience and character, so far as formed, to its full formation, moral vigor and security. The question is often asked, Why evil in the universe? Could not God have prevented it? Undoubtedly He could, confining the world of creation to non-moral and non-accountable beings. Just as pain, the protective of animal organism, could have been excluded in a world of mere physical forces or of vegetable organisms. But as in the animal organism is the necessity of pain, so in the moral is the necessity of personal agency; and in this fact of finite moral agency and its exercise, is the possibility of failure and deviation from right. To be, it must exercise itself; and in such exercise is trial and probation. Innocence is not excellence, the strength and excellence of formed character. The one is the weakness of the infant; the other, the vigor, and power, and security of the full-grown man. Such power and vigor only come, so far as we can see, through moral growth under test and probation. The test of Eden consti-

---

* There is in this account, literally: (*a*) The Divine being, Elohim. (*b*) The human being, Adam and the woman. (*c*) The tempter and the temptation. (*d*) The result of the act of yielding. Act and its results. (*e*) These results: death, woman's condition, conflict of seeds.

These open to question, as figurative: (*a*) Was it a literal serpent? (*b*) Was it a literal serpent only? (*c*) Did Elohim or the serpent speak in words? (*d*) Were the effects physical only through the moral? (*e*) Or were the effects moral through the physical? (*f*) Or did both of these act co-instantaneously?

tuted the divinely given opportunity, with its necessary risks for such growth and maturity. It was the part of Divine wisdom and compassion, even after failure, to bring in remedial agencies; to afford means by which a fallen might become a redeemed race. But to the formation of character, spiritual vigor, moral elevation, strength and security, such probation would seem to have been a necessity.

That test was simple, and mercifully arranged as to its particulars. A certain act was forbidden upon the authoritative word of the Divine Creator and Benefactor. The consequences of disobedience were clearly made known, as the blessing of its opposite implied. It was thus a test of loyalty, of faith in the Divine word and character; and it contained an assurance of welfare in one direction, as of disaster in the other. To forbear was obedience and life; to eat was disobedience and death—was resistance and disregard as to the will of the heavenly Sovereign and Benefactor.

The temptation, as it came, was from without, herein mitigating the nature of the offence. Its form was twofold. First, to self-exaltation and personal benefit: "Ye shall be as God." Second, to disbelief, want of faith in the truth of God: "God doth know that in eating you will not be injured, but rather exalted and benefited; has said to you what is not true." This first temptation, as are all subsequent in their ultimate analysis, was a lie, a slander against God. And faith, not in God, but in the devil, the source of the disobedient act and all its consequences. Morally and spiritually, the fall took place when God was disbelieved and the tempter trusted. The actual eating was the outward and visible sign of the fall as already, inwardly and spiritually, accomplished. Of course, all the moral and spiritual effects were heightened as this inward state found, in the act, its outward expression.

What was its result? Was it entirely moral and spiritual, in its deranging and destructive effects, from within outward, affecting the body, and thus working to its corruptibility and mortality? Or was it entirely bodily, poisoning the body, and from without inward depraving, through the body, the spiritual nature? Or was it both of these combined, the spirit depraved and the body poisoned in one and the same act of transgression? These questions are not specifically answered. Manifestly the predominant feature and result is the spiritual and moral, the sinful act. Derangement and moral death beginning, will soon damage and deprave the body. The divinely announced result includes both—disobedience, moral defection, bodily dissolution, and mortality.

That divinely announced result, both in its matter and order, is deeply significant. While the human offenders are questioned and their extenuation heard, there is no such questioning, no such extenuation with the tempter. He is condemned in his instrument as he is himself, and eventually to a complete overthrow. The woman, as first in the transgression, is put in subjection to the man; is to bring forth in pain and sorrow, and yet is to bring forth eventually the Deliverer. The man is condemned to labor as the condition of existence; and, with the woman, as in him and all his posterity, becomes subject to bodily mortality. In the sentence, as we have seen, there is alleviation. Woman's suffering becomes the medium to the coming of the Deliverer; man's toil is really a protective against various temptations to evil. And, in the intimation of the victorious conqueror of the evil one, was wrapped up the hope of a coming restoration.

With only one other specific point are we just here occupied: the personality of the tempter. The serpent is spoken of, and yet allusions in the New Testament to this serpent indicate something more than the literal serpent: the presence, indeed, of the great enemy. How, it is asked, can this be literal? Which is to be understood? Perhaps the best reply would be, both. If, as the apostle tells us, Satan can transform himself into an angel of light, as he probably transformed himself into man, when he tempted our blessed Lord, he could into a serpent, with the first man. And the subsequent conflict of the literal seed of the woman and the seed of the literal serpent would be part of the result accompanying the spiritual conflict; to terminate in the final victory of the spiritual seed in a higher sphere of operation. Evidently this latter is the predominant one: the overthrow of all enemies, the final triumph of the seed of the woman, in His final heavenly exaltation.

Connected with this subject questions are often

asked, and to which, perhaps, only partial replies can be suggested.

One of these is as to the possible opposite result of the trial—successful probation—to the first man. Would probation have terminated there ; and if so, how would his posterity have been affected ? As in certain respects they fell in him, so if he had stood, would they have stood in him—in other words, have needed no probation ? Scripture does not specifically raise, and therefore does not answer this question. The first man may have needed further trial ; and his posterity, even if he had been successful, and they enjoying its advantages, might have still needed further personal trial to the formation of personal character.

Another of these questions is as to the effect of that trial as successful both with the first man and the race, his posterity. Would the result have been bodily immortality, the non-entrance of bodily death in human experience ? Man's bodily nature, it is urged, is constitutionally mortal, comes under the law of organic dissolution. To this three replies have been made : First, man's bodily nature is so, as that of a sinful being. How, if sinless, is the point of inquiry ? Second, we have only to suppose a different physical organism, one in which the supply is exactly adapted to the demand of the system, so as to go on forever, and the difficulty is removed. Third, earthly existence with the race, as with two exceptional cases, Enoch and Elijah, might terminate, not in bodily death, but in translation, and the transformation needed for another state of existence. There was the implied assurance of continued existence to obedience; but nothing as to its localities and conditions. Evidently the idea of perpetuated life, the possibility of life immortal, is thus implied in the record. This "plank from the wreck of Paradise" thus survived to men's minds as a possibility of human experience.

So, again, the further question has been asked: Was not the fall, and the knowledge in personal experience of good and evil, a stage, and a necessary one, to a higher condition? As "God causes the wrath of man to praise Him," so did He not, in this case, the malignity of Satan? The reply to this is, that as, in the blessed angels and in the humanity of our blessed Lord, there was no knowledge in personal experience of evil, for full and successful trial, and the highest excellence following, so we cannot affirm any such necessity in the case of the first man. Sin is not a God-originated thing or agency. He controls and overrules it, as originating with His finite creatures; but hates and condemns it. How He would have done with man sinless we cannot fully say; but we can say He would have blessed him, and blessed him more highly, than as brought under the power of sin. While, therefore, it cannot be said that man's fall was a needed step to his moral and spiritual elevation, we may say it afforded opportunity for the most conspicuous manifestation and exercise of Divine love and wisdom, to the deliverance of men from the effects and consequences of his transgression, and thus for his moral and spiritual elevation. But that such elevation could not have been without sin is beyond our capacity of affirmation. As it was, in the actual fact, "where sin abounded, grace superabounded." And thus, as sin reigned unto death, so grace, in the Divine work and righteousness, reigned unto eternal life. God thus caused, alike, the malignity of Satan and the sin of man to show forth His praise.

CHAPTER XII.

THE DOCTRINE OF SIN.

Distinction of Original and Actual.—The first original sin.—Ambiguity of the terms employed to describe it.—Scripture assertion of man's sinfulness.—What the nature of this, and its connection with the sin of the first man.—Theories of such connection.

In an ideal world there would be no place for this topic. In the actual it meets us everywhere; not only in systems of theology, but in every-day life; not only in Christianity, but in all forms of religion; in the struggles of human feeling, as in the confessions and speculations of human science and philosophy. Such fact, deeply significant in itself, becomes still more so as in its connection with the teaching of Old and New Testament revelation. This teaching is that of sin as in some manner, either in act or tendency, an inheritance, an experience common to the race. Man is described as a sinful being. The two great questions of Christian theology with reference to it are, what is this sin? how can it be overcome and eradicated? To understand the remedy we must know the evil. As we see the real character of this evil, we see the necessity, and to some degree what must be the character of the effective remedy. We begin with the first, sin.

Here, in the beginning, we encounter the distinction

of original and actual sin. With the former there are many difficulties. With the latter, comparatively few. Actual sin, sin contemplated as an act, is deviation, in the free movement of a moral agent, by commission or omission from the Divine law; wrong-doing, or failure of right-doing as to God, the Supreme Ruler and Lawgiver. Sin is offence against Divine law, as is crime against that which is human. Crimes thus may not be sins, and sins may not be crimes. It was no crime for man and wife, under Roman law, to separate and seek new partners; but it was sin. On the other hand, it was a crime for a Roman soldier to refuse to do religious homage to the effigy of Cæsar; but it was not sin. Both of these words imply a law given by a rightful authority, as also the voluntary agency of those living under it. Transgression of the Divine law is specially described as sin. Such sin in other relations may be and usually is described by other terms—immorality, villainy, dishonesty. Contemplated Godward, they are sins.

Prior, however, to the consideration of actual sins is usually that which is called original. The nomenclature here is not by any means a happy one; and it is to be regretted that the idea of Zwingle, as to the use of some other term, had not been adopted in the confessions of the Reformation. What is really meant could have been better expressed by the word depravity, corruption, or tendency to sin of human nature, and the present entanglement and confusion avoided. Sin, which is a word properly descriptive of a voluntary criminal act, is thus used to describe the involuntary state or condition of the race, as of the agent prior to his capacity of voluntary action. So, in the same manner, guilt, which properly describes the condition into which a voluntary agent brings himself by a criminal act, is used to describe the state or condition of others by such act affected. Original sin, meaning by this the condition in which men are by the sin of the first man, is usually spoken of as preceding actual sin. And yet it was an actual sin of the first man that produced it. Strictly speaking, the original sin, *peccatum originans*, was that of the first man. The effect of this is the depravity, the corruption, the universal race tendency to follow in his footsteps. This, described as *peccatum originatum, originis*, or *originale*, always involves a modification of the sense of *peccatum*. In the first, describing the offence of the first man, it means a voluntary criminal act; in the second, a naturally depraved state or disposition. Refusal or failure to recognize this distinction has been the prolific source of confusion and embittered controversy.

The two points, thus included in this subject of race depravity, or, as usually described, original sin, are, first, the fact as to its existence and nature; second, its connection with the sin and fall of the first man. This fact itself comes out in a twofold form. First, in those passages of Scripture and their implications in which the actual condition of the race is described. Distinction here is not specifically made between actual sin and the race tendency to its commission. But the point of significance is the universality of sin both in space and time; its manifestation under variety of times and circumstances; its manifoldness of operation, and yet, in all, its essential unity of character. Man is contemplated as a sinful being. If this is not a part of his nature, in that nature as related to its surroundings, it is called into existence. Just as diseases in certain families, through several generations, indicate hereditary tendency in such families, so this disease of depravity in the family of the race, in all its generations and under all conditions and circumstances, indicates no less clearly a law of moral and spiritual heredity as its natural explanation. "All," says the apostle, "have sinned and come short of the glory of God." Whether regarded as a result and proof of human depravity, or simply as the outworking of human nature, the fact is substantially the same.

Most startling are some of the illustrations. The first of human born becomes a murderer. The earth, in the course of time, becomes so filled with violence, as to bring upon its guilty inhabitants a flood of destruction. The confusion of Babel, not long after the flood, is the effect of disobedience to the Divine will. In the course of a few generations, the spread of idolatry and polytheism and their abominations necessitate the call of Abraham and his family, as witnesses of the living God, and as protesting against the pollutions and cruelties of heathenism. Even among these chosen people, sin and idolatry are constantly breaking forth, and brought under Divine reproof and punishment. Their history is one long record of Divine blessings perverted, as of Divine penalties inflicted. Even the best specimens of the faithful, how painful the record, how clear the confession from them of failure and sin! It is the race unity of sin that is thus exhibited; of something in human nature, left to itself, going into sin; even, in spite of Divine grace, falling into its commission.

So, too, the world of men is contemplated as needing salvation; and that as divinely provided to meet, not a partial, but a universally existing race necessity. The children of a sinful progenitor are thus participants with him of sin; in the nature, which thus finds expression. What is involved in such participation we examine further on. Just here we note the fact of heredity in natural disposition or constitution: sinful, dying parents, giving birth to mortal and sin-inclined children; giving them the inheritance of mortal bodies, of inward corrupt and depraved tendencies.

Connected scripturally with this fact of the actual condition of the race, and pointing to something in its nature as explanatory of its existence, are scriptural statements as to its connection with the sin of the first man. "As in Adam," says the apostle, "all die, so in Christ shall all be made alive." Christ's life, imparted to the race, is not merely that of bodily life. Preceding this, and a preparative condition to it, is Christ's moral and spiritual life to men morally and spiritually dead, thus in this condition, through connection with the first man. So, too, in the parallel of the fifth chapter of Romans, the two great heads of the race are set over against each other—the one as bringing in sin and death, the other as bringing grace and life to the race. It is the race unity in each of these, its respective heads, that is thus manifestly contemplated. And we thus have the race inheritance of a sin-disposed nature. In the light of such fact we read the confession of the psalmist (Ps. 51 : 5), the language of Job 14 : 4, the conflict described in Rom. 7 : 5-25, as to the indwelling power of the depraved nature ; and the language of our blessed Lord as to the need of spirit birth to the naturally born, for admission to the kingdom of God.

Thus far there has been little of serious difference as to the fact of man as a sinful being—in other words, human depravity, tendency to sin, going out, as human nature is left to itself, into actual sin, as moral capacity for such sin is reached. In this respect, and in some way or other, this fact of race connection and race inheritance, of the fallen nature of the first man, has been generally accepted. The manner of that connection, what it involves in the moral condition of the race, and as to man's standing, under the Divine law, prior to actual sin, has been that of controversy. Without going into the details and stages of this controversy, it will be sufficient to indicate the main point of interest in it—that of the moral and legal standing of the race, as of each member of it prior to actual sin, say that of the new-born infant, through race connection, and from this first sin. Birth connection, natural connection, is of course involved. But in this what is additionally included? Two theories—the participation theory of Augustine and the imputative theory of Anselm, and later scholastic and reformed theologians answered it, by the affirmation of personal guilt, and consequently a positive Divine sentence of condemnation. The first of these theories, under that of realism, affirmed the presence of the race in the person and act of their progenitor; and, therefore, their participation in the consequences of this common act—personal guilt and condemnation. The other found them thus present and participant, not in person, but in that of their divinely appointed representative, the first man, and coming to them in the way of imputation. In both cases the result was the same: the race, each member of the race, criminally guilty of the first sin, and, therefore, under sentence of Divine condemnation.

Connected with these, and ending in the same conclusion, was that of the participation personally in the sin of the first man, not by concurrent act, as with Augustine, not in the act of the representative, as with the later view, but in the malignity of the inherited nature itself, which, wanting in love to God and all good, and full of positive tendencies to evil, was itself sin, and under the divinely condemning sentence. Here the transition from the idea of depravity, a state, to that of sin, an act; from that of guilt as the effect of personal criminality, to guilt as the effect of the criminality of others, was made without distinct recognition. Sin, an act, was made to describe the effect of a depraved and fallen condition; and guilt, in the sense of criminality, was used to describe the effect, in others, of such criminality. In all these theories the personal agent, prior to any act or agency of his own, and even to his capacity of agency or of action, was found guilty, criminally so, of sin, an act, and legally under Divine sentence as to its consequences. Children, in the language of Scripture, "an heritage of the Lord," who "are not able to discern good or evil," are thus made not only to know evil, but to be criminal participants in it, and under its Divine sentence of doom.

This, very naturally, led to the sacramental remedy. For dying infants there could be no other. The sin and its doom, criminally incurred, not by their own act, was, in the same manner, without their act or knowledge, removed. And, as one sacrament thus became debased from its original high moral and spiritual significance into a mere fetich, so, in due time, the other came to be regarded and treated as of similar character. Where sin is looked upon as a physical thing, it will be treated, and its cure sought with physical remedies.

Over against this affirmation of race criminality and condemnation from the first sin is that of its extreme opposite, what has been called the theory of example. Men are affected by Adam's sin through the temptation of his example. Just so far as they are affected by that example, and follow it, just so far are they participants of his fall and its consequences. This ignores the fact of prior participation in these consequences in the result of mortality, and really makes all connection, not that of race or nature, but of actual offence. Actual sin is all that we find in these respects in the human race; in human failure and transgression. We are as was the first man. He sinned and fell. We sin and fall. Adam injured himself; we injure ourselves; are really affected only by his example. Here, manifestly, there is defect of scriptural truth and scriptural statement, as in the previous theories there are superfluities. While, in one direction, man is scripturally held accountable only for his own actions, in another he is exhibited as acting from the impulses of a depraved and fallen nature. He does undoubtedly follow the example of his progenitor; but why so invariably and universally? Why does he need to be born again for his entrance into the kingdom of God? There is the race tendency, the race inheritance. We may not be able fully to explain the fact; but it must be accepted.

One other of these theories—that of the *scientia media*—may be briefly mentioned; the race, as individuals, are accounted and treated as guilty, as it was foreseen they would actually become so. Scripture, it must be said, treats men as offenders, not in view of what they might or may do under certain conditions, but in view of what they have actually done. The question may be asked, Why not include, under this theory, the sin of the first man, as well as those of his children?

Have we, then, any way of stating this connection? There is one that describes it as actually existing; and this, perhaps, is as far as we are capable of going—that of consequence. Human depravity is not identically the sin of the first man. But it is the divinely established consequence, in the race, of that sin; in the Divine overrulings, to manifest not only the Divine justice, but the Divine goodness and wisdom. Analogies to it are to be found in all directions. Heredity has become a familiar word in human science. And there are few communities of any size that do not afford individual and family illustrations. A sinful progenitor will beget depraved offspring. The terrible truth of human sinfulness comes to men everywhere. It is a human, a natural fact. It is natural to man, as he is, in his present condition. This had its beginning with the first sin, and is connected with it. As Christ is the head of the race for its deliverance, so is Adam for its sinfulness. This depraved nature needs to be changed, just as the actual sins, which are its outgoing, need to be pardoned. In the work of Christ, as in the Spirit of Christ, is provision for both of these necessities. In this way we have no confusion of personalities. Each one must give account, not of Adam's, but of his own sin to God. And each finds, in the provisions of Divine grace, that which will enable him to obtain pardon for these his own sins, Divine spiritual influence to the mastery over the effect of Adam's sin, the positive sanctification of his own spiritual nature.

The question has sometimes been raised, in connection with this topic, whether man is to be spoken of as totally depraved. The phrase is not a happy one. It may mean that men are demons, as bad as they are capable of being. This excludes degrees of guilt as varieties of character, and is not of course possible. It is sometimes used to affirm the truth that depravity extends to every part of human nature, not only to the body, but to the intellectual, the rational, the moral, and spiritual nature. This, however true, would be better expressed in other terms. Knapp's definition of depravity "as that tendency to sinful passions, or unlawful propensities, which is perceived in man, whenever objects of desire are placed before him, and laws are laid upon him," gives a much better idea as to its character. (See Rom. 7.)

See on this and chapter preceding, Hodge, Martensen, Müller's "Christian Doctrine of Sin," Harold Browne, and Dr. Buel on "Ninth Article."

CHAPTER XIII.

ACTUAL SIN.

Sin, as a criminal act, has its degrees, of commission and omission.—Involuntary sins; sins of ignorance; voluntary; scandal; sin against the Holy Ghost.

The transition here is to sin in the strict sense of the word; from sin, as something in the nature, to that which is in the act; from sin, as in the race, to that which is in the individual. In this last, as already intimated, there is implied the idea of Divine law promulgated; known or knowable; and the free agency of the human subjects under that law; the free agency of rational and moral being. Transgression, by such being, of the Divine Law is sin, sinful action.

As, moreover, in numberless variation, as to its modes and conditions, under which it is committed, such sin has its degrees of moral quality, as of desert of Divine dealing. The Stoics affirmed that all sins were equal. What, perhaps, they meant was that their quality was the same. So, too, the affirmation has often been made by Christian theologians that, as sin is against an Infinite Being, so it is infinite in its character. But moral acts are not measured in all respects by the character of their object; as to their quality or degree by this object to which they have reference. If so, acts of obedience and service to God would be infinitely excellent. Degrees and kinds of sin, moreover, are expressly spoken of in Scripture, and as to respective consequences. The servant, knowing his Lord's will, and doing it not, is under a heavier penalty and with a greater degree of culpability than his more ignorant fellow-servant, pursuing a like outward course. "He that delivered Me to thee," is the language of the Master to Pilate, "hath the greater sin."

Offence, indeed, against God is deeper and more heinous than as in other directions. But thus, as against Him, it has its variations of degree, as of character.

As, moreover, under law, requiring certain things to be done, as others to be avoided, there is necessarily the distinction of sins of omission and of commission. Question has been raised as to their comparative character. In the general the act of commission is more open and positive, and thus indicates more positiveness of resistance and disobedience. At the same time, there are some sins of omission that are also open and public, and in other respects heinously inexcusable. In individual cases, also, with peculiar light, and advantages, the omission is worse and less excusable than the commission of others, in less favorable conditions. The main point of special interest here is the reality of both of those forms of sin: that omission as well as commission is sin, comes under Divine disapproval and condemnation.

Looking thus at sins as of various degrees, as alike

of commission and of omission, there are certain aspects of them that remain to be noted.

Among these are what have been called involuntary sins; involuntary in the sense that there is not specific deliberation and determination beforehand. The agent finds himself in an unanticipated contingency, is surprised, and acts hastily. He is encountered by a new form of temptation, and overcome; or, through want of watchfulness against old habits, falls under their power. The reality of sin is present in all such cases. The mitigation is with Him who knows all. With such sins in others we must make large allowance. With those of our own we must find out the weakness and defect, and be watchful against their future influence. Every such sin, apart from its other effects and meanings, is a temptation to its future and more deliberate repetition—the seminal principle to many others.

Akin to these are what are called sins of ignorance. Our Lord's prayer on the cross for His enemies pleads their ignorance of the extent of their transgression. So, too, the apostle speaks of what he did "ignorantly and in unbelief." And yet in both is the implication of sinful doing. The acts might have been worse; but the ignorance, or imperfect knowledge, did not entirely remove their sinful character. Such ignorance, if not wilful, might and ought to have been removed by careful inquiry.

More positive are what are called voluntary sins; when the act is known and contemplated as sin, and the determination is to its commission. Here, too, it may be said, the choice is not of the sin, as sin, or for its own sake, but of sin as the condition to the enjoyment or the object for which it is committed. The sin, in such case, is not so much the object as it is the price, the risk to the attainment of something else. The act, in such case, injures its perpetrator. It may injure others. In both of these respects, as in itself, it dishonors God. Its peculiar characteristic is that of its deliberate commission.

When, moreover, such is the case, it will probably be repeated. The act is, itself, a temptation to its repetition. In every such act is the seminal power and principle of a habit. What was thus, at first, sin, an act unarrested, becomes sinful habit, vice, vicious character. There may be a degree beyond this—that of sinning for its own sake. Even, however, in apparent cases of this kind, it may be the association of the act or sin with some kind of enjoyment. Such monstrosity seems to be explained only under this supposition.

And all these forms of sin may be further contemplated as to their objects. They are against God, against the sinner's own moral and spiritual nature, against the interests and welfare of his fellow-men. As related to the agent and his fellow-men, these effects had better be described by other words. It, as they are related God, that they are called sins. What is really wrong in any other direction is a sin against Him; is against His law; is best expressed, in its meaning, as toward Him, by this word sin.

Two other specialties of sinful action may be briefly described. One of these is sins of offence, scandals, by which the innocent, the weak and ignorant may be led astray, or the sinful confirmed in wrong doing. Our Lord speaks of such offences, and of the woe to those through whom they come. And the apostle mentions cases in which even allowable things are indulged in to the injury of others. The doubtful things to others, however clear to the man himself, as innocent and harmless, must be avoided, as the weak brother may be led into the sin with which he associates the act in question. Anything doubtful to the doer himself must be abstained from; and the benefit of all doubt be given to the claims of God. Thus doubting and doing, such a one sins and is condemnable.

The last of these specific distinctions of sins, is that of "blasphemy against the Holy Ghost." The original reference, it will be remembered, was to the blasphemous ascription, by the Scribes and Pharisees, of our Lord's miracles, wrought through the power of the Holy Ghost, to the agency of Satan. The position thus has been taken, as by Chrysostom, that as the conditions cannot be reproduced, so the sin, under others, cannot be repeated. Others, as Augustine, found it to be the sin of persevering resistance to the Holy Spirit; and, therefore, as the sin of all obdurate transgressors. This came to be identified with "the sin unto death," in the Epistle of John; as of that, in the Epistle to the Hebrews, "incapable of being renewed to repentance." So again, in a modified form, the deadly as contrasted with "the venial sins" of mediæval theology. Confining our view to our Lord's language, it seems to describe a particular form of offence, and to imply a crisis in character, as involved in, or as the result of its commission. Men may now, as did the Scribes and Pharisees, blaspheme Christ's works and words filled with the Holy Spirit, and impute them to the agency of Satan. They may do it against as great, if not greater, evidence than was possible to the original offenders. If these essential conditions can be reproduced, the act of which they are the occasion, it would seem, can be reproduced also.

A very common idea of this sin is that of unworthy participation of the Lord's Supper; "eating and drinking to themselves damnation"—the rendering of the Authorized Version—instead of "condemnation." So, too, it has been associated with the refusal, when under deep conviction at revivals, to go up to the mourner's bench to be prayed for. Then, again, with the sin of indulgence in some hidden offence or evil habit; or of resisting Divine influences to a life of religious duty. Every pastor of any experience will encounter such cases. Where there is real anxiety, earnestness, a desire to be free from such power, there are indications of hope that, whatever the real sins and follies of the persons thus anxious, the dreaded state has not been reached. They who really blaspheme and sin against the Holy Ghost have no such troubles. In their induration they have gotten rid of everything of that character.

CHAPTER XIV.

SIN IN ITS CONSEQUENCES.

These in their two aspects, as natural and positive, outward and inward.—Divine penalties.—Chastisement in penalty.—Punishments in present and future world ; wherein positive, wherein natural.

THE definition of sin, already given, wrong-doing as to God, transgression, by commission or omission, of the Divine law, carries with it certain inferences as to its effects and consequences. These are outwardly upon others, as they are outwardly and inwardly upon the sinner himself. Such an act must have its consequences. It is related to the Divine, eternal order of things, and may be eternal in these its consequences. It breaks in upon this Divine order; in so doing, introduces elements of evil and confusion. Some of these consequences, as exhibited in Scripture, we may now examine.

They may be contemplated under two aspects: first, simply, as consequences under the divinely established order of things ; secondly, as penalties under the Divine prerogative and jurisdiction of a Supreme Lawgiver. In both aspects, it is as related to law that they take place. In the former, however, it is simply as natural law, or a naturally operating order or agency. In the latter, we distinctly contemplate the element of personality—personal character in the Lawgiver and Administrator, as also in the offender. In both, moreover, we go back to personality ultimately, as the only rational ground either of the moral law or of the natural order. Taking, therefore, into account this fact of personality, in the Author as in the breaker of the law, we look at it in some of its effects and consequences.

These, to some degree, are indicated in the threefold form in which sin is described—ungodliness, alienation from God; hypocrisy, pretence and self-deception as to God; wickedness, open and positive rebellion against God. Finding in every such manifestation this fact of sin, what in it is always involved? What its effect upon the offender himself, as upon others?

First of all, there is in the act and course of sin the privation and loss of Divine favor, the satisfaction and peace therewith connected. This may not be recognized, or even thought of, by the sinner; but it is no less a real deprivation from that fact. Not to be conscious of such loss is itself a moral calamity. No peace to the godless and sinful, unrest, failure as to the peace and blessedness for which he has the capacity. Naturally connected with this is the anticipation of results opposite; of the positive effects of sin, of violation or failure as to the Divine law. Again, and with these the self-condemning consciousness of wrong-doing as to God—the sense of Divine disapproval and displeasure, the anticipation of Divine penalty. In the mean time is going on the retributive operation of the law of habit; the sinful act becoming the sinful habit, the vice; and mastering capacity and power of resistance. Some of these effects may be modified by others. The fears and anticipations, for instance, of conscience may be silenced in the result of moral insensibility and induration. But the latter is the worse condition of the two, and is wanting in all real peace and satisfaction. So far as regards what may be called its present, natural results, sin, in the experience of the sinner, is wretchedness, want of satisfaction and real peace—often positive suffering and misery.

And as there are these inward effects of sin upon the sinner himself, so, in many cases, there are others of an outward character, affecting the health, the bodily comfort, the social and moral condition of the sinner, as of those by whom he is surrounded; upon the members of his family, upon his associates in business and otherwise, upon the community. The act, or course of sin, as we have seen, is against, is one of wrong relation to the sinner's own moral nature, as to that of God and that of his fellow-creatures. It is, thus, against the righteous, wise, and beneficial order of things. It produces confusion, injures the sinner, does mischief to others, and dishonors God. Whether in what we call the way of natural consequence or of divinely administered law, these are the wages, the effect of sin. And, beyond this, is the revelation of the Divine word, of consequences in the future, the consequences of sin beyond this world, in a future state of existence. "The wages of sin is death." It is death of the body. If unarrested, it is death of the moral and spiritual nature. If this, the death beyond of coming retribution.

Divine Punishment.

We thus approach the question of the Divine purpose, and object, in dealing thus with offenders and offences against Divine law. In other words, why are there Divine penalties? Why, it may be asked, as helping us to a reply to this question—why do we punish criminals in this world? The reply of some is, to reform the criminal. Some say, to deter others from like courses. Some, to protect the innocent. Some, to uphold the sacredness and majesty of the law. All these answers are, to a certain degree, and with reference to certain cases, correct; but they are all partial. And they may leave out the main element, in view of which punishment is inflicted, and that by which alone it is justified—the criminality of the person punished. When Caiaphas said that "one man should die and the nation not perish," this fact, if not implied, was not distinctly stated. If he had said one innocent man, his argument would have probably shocked some even of his hearers. So, again, when an English judge told a thief that he was hanged, not for horse-stealing, but that horses might not be stolen, it was an admission that the penalty was not justified by the offence. All these other objects—the reformation of the criminal, the protection of society, the sacredness of the law—may and must have their place. But, along with these, and always, must be the fact of criminality and the proportion of the penalty to the crime. The offender against Divine law, and, therefore, as deserving of penalty, is the subject of Divine administration and dealing. God is justified as He speaks, clear as He judges; and this in view of the real nature of the acts decided upon.

Contemplating sin as thus divinely dealt with, and from its first commission, we approach a topic of deep interest in connection with this whole subject—the difference between Divine punishment and Divine chastisement and discipline. The element of penalty, to some degree, runs through it all, and yet it may be mainly chastisement. Manifestly this is the aspect of the Divine dealings with the penitent and forgiven transgressor, especially in connection with natural sufferings from his past sins, bodily or otherwise. So, too, to some degree, with such offender in the earlier stages of his course; with many, perhaps with all, to some degree during their earthly probation. Just as the bodily man is warned in his very structure against certain bodily acts and habits, so is the moral and spiritual in the laws and operations of his moral and spiritual organism. "God is not willing that any should perish." He would have all to be saved and come to repentance. His dealings with the sinner are, at the first, to warn him against sin; at a more advanced stage to turn him from it to repentance. When and where chastisement and discipline terminate in penalty, it may be difficult to decide. Chastisement, indeed, as already intimated, usually involves a degree of punishment; and yet it may be considered only as chastisement. In the experience of the forgiven and repentant transgressor already alluded to, struggling painfully with his old habits and suffering thus from such habit, there is something of penalty. At the same time, it is merciful and loving chastisement, warning him against indulgence and helping him in his onward course. In all such cases we see the two elements in their combined operation.

But there is a point in contemplation, and a stage in the course of the offender against Divine law, when chastisement, discipline, terminates; when the offender is contemplated as coming under punishment. Such Divine punishment may be in the present life. It may be in the future. If the disciplinary element disappear in the present life, it is not so ordinarily. Here we are spoken of and dealt with as on trial, probation. For full and final results, either of reward or of punishment, we are pointed to the future. But whether present or future, this fact of sin, in its punishment, is clearly exhibited, as under the Divine dealing, "God will judge the world in righteousness."

What will be, or is, the nature of such punishment we cannot fully comprehend. The fact that it is in a world of spirit or of spiritualized bodies, and beyond the conditions of our temporal experience, makes it thus difficult of comprehension. Contemplating it negatively as that of deprivation of blessing, positively as that of remorse and self-condemnation and suffering, we may briefly look at some of the questions that have been raised in connection with this subject. They demand careful consideration.

One of these questions is, whether Divine punishment in a future world is to be spoken of as only natural, or as both natural and positive. One of the difficulties in its settlement is in the ambiguity of this word natural; changing, in this fact, the meaning of the other word, positive. Natural, with many, means physical, and nothing more. In such usage, positive would be moral personality. Natural, again, as opposed to positive, is that which is the result of the established order and operation of the laws of the universe; positive, as something in the Divine will, or working additional. The former, as obligatory, springs out of our natural constitution as related to the natural order of things; the latter, as revealed in Divine law or precept. But the difficulty here is the impossibility, in actions and courses, of carrying out this distinction. We do know that there are duties naturally and positively revealed. But the natural duties are insisted upon in revelation; and the revealed duties, if we understood nature more fully, might be recognized as, by that nature demanded—in other words, as natural. What, in a lower stage of human progress, may be positive, in a higher and subsequent stage may be seen as natural or moral. Natural punishments, in this sense, would be those that are the result of the divinely established constitution of things; positive, those that are result of Divine volition and action specifically revealed. But then, again, the latter, if we fully understood the divinely established constitution, might be seen to be included in it. The positive, in such case, might be recognized as natural.

Our only use, therefore, of this distinction is as related to our capacity of knowledge. There are naturally known duties. There are duties that are positively revealed. There are rewards and punishments of both of these classes. In this sense, as positively revealed, Divine punishments are positive. Our affirmation of them rests upon the revealed word of positive dictation. In this sense they are positive. As to their relation to the established principles of operation for the universe, they may be what we call natural, or, more properly perhaps, moral. "The judgments of Jehovah are right."

Closely connected with this, and one of the issues of our time, is that of the termination of Divine penalty; and with it that of probation beyond the present life. Does the Old or New Testament, in speaking of the punishment of the wicked beyond this world, speak of it as coming to an end? Does it, in speaking of human probation, intimate that such probation may go on in a future state of existence? Reasons may be suggested why such topics should not have been dwelt upon; but the simple issue with which we are concerned is the actual fact of the case. If there is termination to the punishment of the finally impenitent, we are not told of it; the intimations are, rather, the direct opposite. If there be probation for the heathen, or certain classes, it is not revealed. And as we are told to work out our own salvation, so are we required, as we are able, to urge and aid all others in doing.

Two other questions in this matter remain to be noted. One of these has to do with the subjects of Divine penalty. Is their condition simply and only one of suffering? This is frequently asserted. So, too, as to the other assertion, so often made, that such condition of suffering, as of sinfulness, is in constant process of increase and aggravation. Can it be affirmed that this is the teaching of Scripture, or in accordance with the analogy of the Divine dealings in other respects? Sin will be punished according to its real character and deserts, and its consequences have no revealed termination. This is clear. Is it safe or wise, in our ignorance, to affirm anything beyond or additional?

So, again, as to the Divine relations to the subjects of such penalty. It is that of Judge. But is it that only? Is not the Judge also a Father? The relation of all the Divine perfections to this truth of Divine penalty must be borne in mind. Too frequently, if not ordinarily, such penalty and its state are spoken of as related simply and only to justice—God, as Sovereign, holding in supreme right legislative, judicial, and executive powers, and exercising them justly in righteousness; but this, let us remember, is in connection with His other perfections. God cannot undeify Himself. And in all His doings, even in what He calls "His strange work" of penalty, there are workings also of wisdom, of goodness, of infinite love and compassion. In the punishment of the offender the interests of others are provided for, and the condition of the criminal offender, we may say, is the best of which he is capable. In this blackness of the darkness of sin and its consequences, the only light is in the perfections of Him by whom all is administered. In His hands, overruling all and overruling for good, we leave the destinies of His creatures.

CHAPTER XV.

SALVATION FROM SIN.

Modes in which its necessity recognized, and sought.—Sacrifices.—Self-inflicted penalty.—Repentance and restitution.—The Divine provision.—Relation to it of different Persons of the Trinity.—The manifestation of the Person of the Redeemer.—His modes of working.—Position of His death and sufferings.

OVER against these facts of sin and its consequences, manifested in our nature and specifically revealed in Scripture, is that which gives Christianity its peculiar characteristic and name—that of Gospel, God's story or message of salvation. Intimations of this are to be found in the Old Testament. And whether from these or from its own spiritual constitution, human nature, outside the circle of God's chosen people, has looked and striven for it. Sin is something that human nature, in the clear conviction of its existence, cannot rest under with satisfaction. It will either try to make it out not sin, or in some way to get rid of it and its threatened evils. Very briefly some of these forms of effort may be indicated.

One is that of sacrifice. Whether divinely instituted for the first man or not, they were undoubtedly used from the beginning ; were offered by Cain and Abel ; accepted in the case of Abel ; thus accepted as offered during the patriarchal ages; and were put under Divine sanction and direction in the Mosaic dispensation. And in both stages, the ante-Mosaic and the post-Mosaic, these sacrifices were, some of them, of an expiatory character, relieving the criminal from the consequences of his sinful action. Many sacrifices were not thus expiatory. Some of them were thank offerings, some of communion in worship before God. Some of them were propitiative, not necessarily in view of sin or Divine displeasure, but propitiative gifts to secure Divine favor. And then there was the propitiative sacrifice of the subject under the Divine Ruler's displeasure, seeking His pardon and restored favor. Here the propitiative partakes of the nature of the expiative, the sacrifice or gift restitutive, which in its effort endeavors to make satisfaction for the offence and its effects. These are all under the Mosaic law. Ordinarily, too, the expiative preceded the others, and was needed as rendering these others acceptable. In other words, under Divine direction and in a divinely established dispensation, we find expiative sacrifices for sin.

But, as hinted in their promulgation, and as clearly declared, by the prophets of the Old Testament and the teachers of the New Testament, these sacrifices of themselves had no power to take away sin. Their efficacy was in the Divine appointment; the pledge in it given, that if offered in the right spirit and manner they would be acceptable and efficacious. They were types, symbolic prophecies, of a greater and more perfect sacrifice; but of themselves could not take away sin. If, moreover, thus helpless, even as divinely appointed, much more so under the darkness and debasement of heathen idolatry.

The same, too, is to be said as to other supposed modes of expiation for sins. Self-inflicted penalty, for instance; sacrifice of property, of comfort, of children, of life itself, all fail here. The criminal cannot be the judge, jury, executioner, and remitter of penalty in his own case. This could not be under imperfect human law, much less under that which is Divine.

So, too, as to the expiative effects of repentance, restitution as far as possible, and the course of obedience to Divine law following. These are demanded in Scripture, as in reason, and they should be striven for; but, as a matter of fact, they are imperfect as they go on in the present and the future, and they do not at all provide for the delinquencies of the past. They are accepted under the Old Testament, as connected with the divinely appointed modes of sacrificial remission; and they are accepted in the New Testament, as sanctified, and made efficacious through the great sacrifice. Of themselves they cannot take away sin. Human nature, as helpless in such exigency, needs something additional—a special Divine provision for the removal of sin and its consequences; a special Divine assurance as to its manner of application and its efficacy.

That needed provision is a Divine salvation; one administered by a divinely appointed Saviour and Mediator. "There is one Mediator between God and

Man, the Man Christ Jesus." "Jesus Christ came into the world to save sinners." "I came," is Christ's own declaration—"I came to call sinners to repentance."

That provision, as already noted, is Divine. It is one which manifests Divine love and compassion; at the same time, Divine righteousness and wisdom. In the persons of the adorable Trinity we are told of their respective operation. The Father, in love, sends and gives; the Son, in such love, comes, and works, and suffers; the Spirit reveals, and applies, and makes efficacious their agency in its human results and operations. The first of these, as exhibited in Scripture declaration, first naturally claims attention.

This comes before us in various forms of affirmation: "God," says the apostle, "commendeth His love toward us, in that, while we were yet sinners, Christ died for us" (Rom. 5:8). "He spared not His own Son, but delivered Him up for us all" (Rom. 8:32). So in that of St. John: "Herein is love not that we loved God, but that He loved us and gave His Son to be a propitiation for our sins" (1 John 4:9, 10). "God so loved the world, that He gave His only begotten Son" (John 3:16. See also Eph. 2:4–7; Titus 3:4–7; 2 Cor. 5:19). Here are the two great truths as to the salvation of the Gospel: divinely originated; thus originated in love, in undeserved compassion. "God rich in mercy, for His great love wherewith He loved" men, thus providing for their salvation.

As to the work of the blessed Spirit, the examination of this more properly follows that of the Divine

Son of God—the manifestation of God in the person and work of His well-beloved Son. We thus look at this manifestation as presented in the New Testament.

This comes before us in two aspects: First, as it is contemplated in its Divine origination, in the loving self-sacrifice and abasement of the Son of God; secondly, that in which it actually went on in the work of redemption. The first of these is exhibited in Phil. 2:5-10; Heb. 2:14-17; 1:3. In these and similar passages the saving Deliverer is contemplated prior to His earthly manifestation; fulfilling the Father's loving purpose with reference to men; and yet, in so doing, working out His own work of boundless grace and compassion—the Son of God becoming Son of Man for man's deliverance and salvation.

But this Divine purpose, and its manifestation, in the person of the Divine Deliverer, went on in a certain way. His actual manifestation was in His humanity. "He was born of the Virgin Mary;" although supernaturally conceived, yet naturally born. "He increased in wisdom and stature;" was subject to His earthly parents, partook of the circumstances of their earthly condition. He hungered and thirsted, slept and ate, was subject to weariness and pain, and entered into all the forms of sinless life with those around Him; and, at last, in His bodily nature, suffered a violent death. His own self-selected and most common appellation was that of Son of Man. Whatever else, therefore, is to be found in the person of this divinely revealed Saviour is this truth of His humanity. Jesus was a man, in perfect sympathy with man; thus capable of loving and being loved with human affection; capable of being relied upon in His human love, and compassion, and sympathy.

But this Man, thus manifested, in His life, and feelings, and words, and acts, affirmed, and was supernaturally sustained in it by His works, that He was One sent from God; One having a Divine commission; that He was, moreover, not only, as others had been, a prophet, but that He was *The* Prophet; that He was the Messiah, the Christ of Old Testament prediction. He was, thus, the saving Deliverer that was to come into the world. He, Jesus, was the Christ. These two names, now conjoined as a personal appellation, were not so in the beginning. The one was a proper name, the other an official title. Jesus, the divinely sent Teacher, taught and proclaimed that He was the Christ, the Messiah.

Thus far we are in the range not only of human apprehension, but of comprehension. But beyond this is another truth, in the personality of this revealed Saviour, of transcending interest, and of the most overwhelming character: "He is the Son of God," and this in a sense unique and peculiar. Angels and good men are sometimes spoken of as sons of God, as representing or manifesting God's perfections; magistrates as representing His authority. In one case the term is applied to Adam as not born, but divinely called into existence. So too it was the title of the promised Messiah. As applied to Jesus Christ, it includes all these and much more. He is a Son, as, like the angels and good men, manifesting God's perfections. He is a Son of God, as, like the human magistrate, manifesting the Divine authority. He is a Son of God, like Adam, supernatural in His coming into our world. He is, moreover, as Messiah, the Son of God as God, as having a Divine nature, possessed of Divine perfections. While He has a perfect human nature, He has also, in union with it, a Divine nature. The manner of this union we are not told; we have indeed no comprehension. One of the factors to it is infinite. We are incapable of construing this in its distinct essential existence, much less in its union with humanity. What, however, is clear is the truth of the two natures; the perfection of their union, the integrity of each in that union; a heavenly mystery, but full of significance in its earthly and human bearings.

This truth, thus divinely transcendent, at the same time reaches to and meets our deepest necessities. Christ, the Son of Man, is in full sympathy with man. Christ, the Son of God, gives efficacy to that sympathy. While "in all points tempted like as we are," yet " in Him dwells all the fulness of the Godhead bodily." Jesus, the Son of Man, is Christ, the Son of God. "I and My Father are one," is His own language. "Being," said the apostle, "in the form of God, He thought it not a thing to be retained or grasped, to be equal with God." "My Lord and my God," is the unrebuked language of Thomas. "He made Himself to be equal with God." In these and various other declarations we find this truth exhibited—Jesus not only a human, but a Divine Saviour. In the perfect union of these two natures He works for the redemption of men.

CHAPTER XVI.

EFFICACY OF CHRIST'S SUFFERINGS.

Teaching, Example, Suffering.—Position of this last in Scriptural declaration.—Forms of statement in regard to it.—Resurrection.—Intercession.

In dealing with this subject, there are different aspects in which it may be contemplated. The order in which Christ's manifestation was actually made is the most natural, and will best enable us to take in its meaning as a whole. He is represented as a Mediator: thus mediating in various respects; as a Teacher or Prophet; as an atoning Peacemaker or Priest sacrificing Himself; as a conquering and supreme Lord of His redeemed Church and people, and finally over even His enemies. His manifestation for this begins with His instruction as a Teacher. He taught, thus, by word and by example. In that teaching is provision for the necessities of man's intellectual nature; his wants as a rational being; redemption for that part of human nature. Sin affects every part of that nature; and it is only the truth that makes free. The teaching of Jesus by word was very largely as to what was the true character of God; how He regards and treats man; and how, therefore, man ought to treat and honor Him. Every such item of teaching, as to

God, is a revelation of duty to man. The Father in heaven, with a Father's heart of care and love, is thus an object of filial confidence and affection. So too these children of a common Father must also love and benefit each other.

The teaching thus in word was further enforced and illustrated by action. "Jesus went about doing good;" not only teaching, but doing. His miracles and works of compassion for the diseased and the suffering were as object lessons, enforcing what, in that teaching, had been exhibited. The same may be said as to the spirit of His life, thus exhibited and illustrated. In His intercourse with those around Him, not only with His friends, but His enemies, the full meaning of His words became manifest. All that men need to know, all the necessities of man's rational and intellectual nature, are met and provided for in Christ's teaching and life example. In the light of this revelation, of truth, and obligations, and duties, and the way of meeting them, no man to whom they come fails or perishes through lack of knowledge.

But there is one part of this teaching that needs to be emphasized—that which makes known that something more than teaching and example are needed for human redemption. Jesus, the Teacher, in His teaching proclaims and announces Himself as Jesus the redeeming Saviour, not only from the defilement and power, but from the divinely condemning sentence of sin. The whole saving work of Christ is sometimes asserted to consist in this, His teaching and example; by precept and by action. To this the reply has been properly given, that such is not made the case in the New Testament. His teaching and example are spoken of as to be followed, but not as saving men. Saved men are to follow them. They are thus saved by His work; by His sufferings and death. Accordant with this are His own declarations. These come in a twofold form: first, in the specific declarations as to His own death and suffering in relation to the remission of sins. The necessity of the cross was a necessity of human nature—a necessity in the experience and work of the Saviour of human nature. The teaching of Christ, so far from constituting the atoning work or taking the place of His atoning sacrifice, exhibits its peculiar necessity and character; that it is something additional to and different from mere instruction. In that teaching He reveals Himself as a forgiver of sin, as obtaining forgiveness of sins.

Coincident with these specific declarations, as to such necessity, are those of Christ's teaching, as to men's relations to God, their duties arising therefrom, and the spirit in which they must receive performance. Here there is an enlargement, a length, and breadth, and depth, and height of obligation, of duty, and of motive to its performance, upon all that had previously existed. The offender against Divine law, under the Ten Commandments, and condemned, is still more hopelessly condemned in that of the Sermon on the

Mount, as of similar instruction following. If Jesus were only a moral teacher, He enlarged the circle of human obligations, leaving men without capacity of meeting them. The purity and perfection of this teaching as to human duty, make manifest the need to human nature, of some new power for its successful performance; for pardon and help, in case of transgression and failure.

The manner of this efficacy we examine farther on. Just now we look at the truth of the incarnate Christ, in His sufferings and death, for the sins of the world. What this fully involved—in other words, an exhaustive theory of the atonement—will ever baffle the capacities of our finite intellect. Analogies in Divine and human dealings help us to understand it, in its practical bearing, as in its appeal to our affection and sense of obligation. It is a revealed truth; and, as thus revealed, we receive it upon the Divine dictation. In the instruction of Jesus, as we have seen, there is provision for the wants of man's rational nature. Here there is necessity of and provision for his moral nature, his conscience—that of the pardon of sin, the removal of its penalty. We thus turn to some of the declarations of Scripture upon this subject.

Among these, as of special significance, are those in which this part of Christ's manifestation and work is spoken of as in comparison with others. Its position is thus made one of supreme pre-eminence. "As Moses lifted up the serpent in the wilderness, even so must the Son of Man be lifted up" (John 3 : 14). "If

I be lifted up from the earth, I will draw all men unto Me" (John 12 : 32). "My blood shed for the remission of sins" (Matt. 26 : 28). "The Son of Man came to give His life a ransom for many" (Mark 10 : 45). "I delivered unto you, first of all, that Christ died for our sins" (1 Cor. 15 : 2). "We preach Christ crucified" (1 Cor. 1 : 23). "I determined not to know anything among you save Jesus Christ and Him crucified" (1 Cor. 2 : 2). "God forbid that I should glory save in the cross of our Lord Jesus Christ" (Gal. 6 : 14). "We were reconciled to God by the death of His Son" (Rom. 5 : 10). "We have redemption by His blood" (Eph. 1 : 7). "The blood of Jesus Christ cleanseth from all sin" (1 John 1 : 7). "He bore our sins in His own body upon the tree" (1 Pet. 2 : 24 ; 3 : 18). "Christ suffered for sins, the just for the unjust, that He might bring us to God" (Rev. 5 : 9-12). "Thou wast slain, and hast by Thine own blood redeemed us to God." "Worthy is the Lamb, that was slain to receive power, and riches, and wisdom." The point of interest in passages of this character, and taken together, is, first, the number and frequency of their appearance ; secondly, the prominent and central position which they are made to occupy. It is not only Jesus the Christ, the Messiah ; not only Christ the Teacher, the Example ; not only the Master, the incarnate Son of God ; but Christ crucified. All these other truths of His person are exhibited and emphasized. But, as heightening their importance, and along with them, that Christ suffered and died for sinners ; that, as related to the fact of sin and its forgiveness, these His sufferings had atoning efficacy.

Under these general statements, however, are certain particulars—special forms in which this same truth is exhibited. Bearing in mind the usage of such words as redemption, $απολυτρωσις$, remission, $αφεσις$, passing over, $παρεσις$, as to sins with which men are chargeable, and from the consequence and power of which they are delivered by Christ's death, let us notice these particulars of Scripture affirmation.

First, then, are those which connect Christ and His work with forgiveness of sin. The implication everywhere is that men are by nature and act sinful; and, therefore, need not only light and help in other respects, but pardon, forgiveness of sin. One of these classes, to take Knapp's order, is that which affirms that Christ has atoned for our sins. 1 John 2 : 1, 2, " If any man sin ;" Heb. 1 : 3, " By Himself He purged our sins ;" Heb. 9 : 26, " He appeared to put away sin by the sacrifice of Himself." See whole chapter.

Second, we find the same truth in those which require unlimited trust and confidence in Him, and His work of atoning suffering, for Divine acceptance and welfare. Rom. 5 : 1, 2, " Being justified by faith, we have peace with God ;" Eph. 1 : 7, " We have redemption through His blood ;" Acts 26 : 18, " To receive remission of sins by faith in Me."

Third, in those teaching that this is the only divinely revealed way of such forgiveness. Acts 4 : 12, " No other name given under heaven among men, whereby they may be saved;" Heb. 10 : 26, "There remaineth no more sacrifice for sin." See also Heb. 5 : 4.

Fourth, in those teaching that God, through Christ, forgives sin. Acts 10 : 43, "Whosoever believeth in Him shall receive forgiveness of sin." See also Acts 13 : 38, 39. Forgiveness of sins through Him not remissible by Mosaic law. 1 John 2 : 12, "Your sins forgiven for His sake;" Rom. 5 : 10, "Reconciled to God by the death of His Son;" 1 Thess. 1 : 10, "Jesus who delivered us from the wrath to come;" 2 Cor. 5 : 21, "God hath made Him who knew no sin to be sin for us;" Rom. 3 : 21-28, "But now the righteousness of God," etc.; Isa. 53 : 5, "He was wounded for our transgressions," etc.; Ps. 40 : 6, 7, "Sacrificed and offering Thou wouldst not." "Lo I come."

But there are other passages in which the efficacy of Christ's work is more specifically connected with His sufferings and death. Many of those already quoted imply this, as seen from the connection. At the same time, there are others in which it is more specifically affirmed.

First, then, are passages which affirm that Christ suffered and died for all sins—for all the sins of men. Matt. 26 : 28, "My blood shed for the remission of sins;" Rom. 3 : 25, "Whom God hath set forth to be in His blood a propitiation;" 1 Cor. 15 : 3, "Christ died for our sins;" Heb. 9 : 12, "By His own blood He obtained for us redemption." See also 2 Cor. 5 : 14, 15; 1 Pet. 3 : 18; Isa. 53 : 5; 1 John 1, etc.

Just here we encounter the question as to the significance of one of the prepositions employed, ὑπέρ, whether when rendered "for," it is to be taken as "for the advantage of" or "in the place of." The three others, περί with genitive, διά with the accusative, and ἀντί with genitive, present little of material for question. Ὑπέρ, it is affirmed, means "for the advantage of," and nothing more; and, therefore, there is no affirmation here of Christ's suffering in the place of the sinner. To this the reply is twofold. Even supposing such to be the case, the use of ἀντί, and in one instance as compounded with λύτρον, ἀντίλυτρον, "for" sins gives us this idea of substitution. Still further, and apart from the use of ἀντί altogether, the proper rendering of ὑπέρ, in certain connections, is that of "in the place of." "To die, or speak for, or on behalf of another, when the alternative is, that this other shall die or speak himself, is to die or speak in his stead." * This is a grammatical principle. It is thus so because it is one of reason and common sense. See, as illustrative, Rom. 5:7, 10; 1 Pet. 3:18.

The same truth is exhibited when it is said that Christ bore our sins, that He took them upon Himself, that in His death He was treated as a sinner. John 1:29, "The Lamb of God that taketh away the sin of the world;" 1 Pet. 2:24, "He bore our sins in His own body upon the tree; by whose stripes ye are healed;" Heb. 9:28, "Christ once offered to bear the sins of many;" Isa. 53.

---

* Harrison on Greek preposition, with illustrations, p. 462.

So, too, in those in which He is treated as a sinner; and this with reference to our forgiveness. 2 Cor. 5:21, "God hath made Him who knew no sin to be sin for us;" Gal. 3:13, "Christ hath redeemed us from the curse of the law, being made a curse for us."

So, too, in those which speak of His death as a ransom. 1 Tim. 2:6, "He gave Himself a ransom for all," Ἀντιλύτρον ὑπέρ πάντον; Matt. 20:28, "To give His life a ransom for many;" Heb. 9:12, "By His own blood He obtained for us eternal redemption."

Last of all are those in which the death of Christ is compared, in its significance, with those under the Mosaic institute, especially as efficacious, once for all, and not needing repetition. Eph. 5:2, "He gave Himself an offering for us to God—a sacrifice;" Rom. 3:25, "Set forth to be a propitiation;" Heb. 9:14, "The blood of Christ who offered Himself without spot to God;" 1 Pet. 1:19, "As of a lamb slain;" 1 John 1:7, "The blood of Jesus which cleanseth from all sin;" Rev. 5:9-12, "Thou wast slain, and hast redeemed us by Thy blood." "Worthy is the Lamb that was slain;" John 1:29, "The Lamb of God, that taketh away the sin of the world."

In these different forms, not only of Pauline, but of Petrine and Johannean statement, is described that part of the work of the incarnate Christ, included under His sufferings and death, as also its effect upon men in their condition of sin. It is efficacious to the removal of this sin. It first secures pardon to the sinner, as under penalty of the Divine law. It thus, further, through this, appeals to his gratitude and love, and gives him motive and power of deliverance from its enslavement and dominion. In both of these respects the blood of Jesus Christ cleanseth from sin ; and never in one without the other. The former is first emphasized in these passages. The latter more fully comes up in connection with the work of the Blessed Spirit. Confining our attention, for the present, to this former, that of the effect of Christ's sufferings and death, as related to the pardon of sinners, their acquittal or justification under Divine law, we find, first, that they are spoken of in their efficacy as universal. "He died for all." His death is potentially, if not actually, efficacious for all men, in all times ; for the whole life of man ; for every form and degree of sin to which it may be applied. It does not save the blasphemer, who calls it the work of Satan. It does not save the apostate, who turns from it and tramples it under foot. In other words, its remedial power comes in its application, and as it is sought ; cannot be exercised as rejected. But to all trying it, to all accepting and applying it, in good faith, it is in good faith offered, in Divine power, will prove itself efficacious.

Resurrection.

Following the teaching and example of Christ and His atoning sacrifice for sin is the truth of His resurrection. In this we have the triumphant conclusion of His work, the triumphant manifestation of its power and efficacy ; as, also, the vindication of all His claims, whether preceding or following. In the resurrection of Jesus of Nazareth, and the manifestations of the next forty days following, as in the ascension closing these, is evidence not only to the actual spectators, but to those examining their testimony, and to the end of time, of His Divine power and authority; of the validity of all His claims; of the truth of all His words, whether of promise or of warning. To use the expression of the apostle at Athens, "God hath given assurance of Christ's supreme judgeship, and consequently of the validity of all His claims, in that He hath raised Him from the dead." The resurrection is thus made the evidential keystone of the Christian system. As having this position, the apostles are described in the peculiarity of their office as witnesses of it—the event by which was divinely authenticated all the claims and affirmations of the risen and ascended Master. See Rom. 4:25; 7:11; 1 Pet. 1:3; 1 Thess. 4:14; 1 Cor. 15.

Following in the order of thought, and as one of the truths of Christ's state of exaltation, is that of His intercession—His intercessory agency for the welfare of His people. This feature of His work had its place during His state of humiliation, and in His ministry on earth. The prayer of intercession on the night before the crucifixion, strikingly of this character, was doubtless but one of many similar, in His ministry preceding. In these earlier instances, it was the intercession of the well-beloved Son, Himself identified in His trial of human condition with the objects of His petitions. In those following the ascension, it is that of the successful Conqueror of sin and death, the triumphant and exalted Lord, at the right hand of the Father, putting forth His sympathy, exercising His prerogative, and working with the Father for the benefit and welfare of the objects of His affection. "If," says the beloved disciple, "if any man sin, we have an Advocate with the Father; and He is the propitiation for our sins." The idea here seems to be that of the permanent efficacy of His propitiative work; His presence, as such a propitiation, involves the pleading and its efficacy. "Who," again, is the language of St. Paul, "who is He that condemneth? It is Christ that died; yea, that is risen again, who also maketh intercession for us." Here, again, the intercession is contemplated, as having efficacious application, as against all condemning agencies; all such condemnation taken away, in the application to the soul of His atoning sacrifice for sin. "He entered," says the writer of the Epistle to the Hebrews, "into heaven to appear for us" in our behalf "in the presence of God." He is able to save to the uttermost all that come to God by Him; seeing He ever liveth to make intercession for them." The idea, it may be said, in all these passages, is that of Christ's continued mediation for His people—His presence with the Father, in the pleading application of His work in its all sufficiency; in the bestowment and dispensation of His Spirit, to the necessities of His Church and people. Thus, at the right hand of the Father, He is working and overruling to the advancement of His own, as of the Father's purposes; the completion and perfection of His kingdom. He, the great High Priest, touched with a feeling of our infirmities, is, at the same time, the All Powerful Divine Son and Intercessor for all needed assistance and blessing.

CHAPTER XVII.

THE ATONING MEDIATION.

Wherein does it consist.—The theory of example and sympathy, that of judicial satisfaction, that of governmental administration, that of paternal sovereignty.

In looking at the different features of this work, of the Divine-Human Mediator, His teaching and example, His sufferings and death, His resurrection and intercession—in other words, at what may be called His prophetic and priestly, as introductory to His kingly office, we are encountered, in the second, with the deeply interesting question as to the manner of His atoning mediation, the real place and significance of His sufferings and death, in the economy of redemption. That they are our example is undoubted. But they are something more. They are involved to some degree in His identification by sympathy and otherwise with human nature. But this is not all. They are manifestly contemplated in the New Testament as a transaction under law, and as related to forgiveness of sin and removal of its penalty. God is a party in this transaction, as is the suffering Saviour, and those for whom He is described as suffering. There is a Sovereign, there are criminals, and there is a Mediator. What is the atonement or mediative process of reconciliation, through which the Divine Sovereign pardons and accepts the human criminal? in other words, through which comes forgiveness of sins?

Putting aside the early notion of some of the Fathers, that the redemption thus made was one from the dominion of Satan, a ransom or ground of rightful release from his claims or service; as also that already disposed of in the texts quoted, that of Christ's example in suffering and teaching, as constituting His atoning sacrifice for sin, we look at some others of a different character.

One of these is that which finds this atoning work almost entirely, if not purely, one of justice—in what may be called the judicial theory. Under it is the principle of exact equivalence, of strict imputation. The righteous Judge identifies the Mediator with the criminal. By imputation of the sin of the criminal, the Mediator becomes guilty, not merely in the sense of participant in the consequences, but of the criminality itself; as is the criminal, by like imputation of merit, participant of the Mediator's righteousness, not only of its benefits, but of its reality and merit. Along with this, of strict imputation, as demanded by perfect justice, is that of exact equivalence. The Mediator suffers all that the criminal deserved, and all that he would have suffered; the criminal, imputatively identified with his Mediator, has the desert of that Mediator's righteousness. To such a one, as thus identified with Christ, there is not only pardon, but perfect righteousness.

Here is the twofold difficulty of Omniscience—perfect knowledge, seeing and knowing beings and things as they are not, as also a hopeless confusion of personalities. Sufficient to say, that while bringing out one truth—that of Divine justice—it does not take account of others, exhibited in Scripture in connection with this atoning work; as with some of these it is in manifest conflict.

Intended to assert this same truth of the Divine justice, so emphasized in the judicial theory, as also others, is that which has been called the governmental or administrative. Here, the Divine Sovereign is contemplated not simply as in the judicial, but in the executive capacity, the Supreme Ruler, in whose person is combined all the functions of perfect government. The problem, therefore, in such Divine administration, and even in regard to penalty, is not simply its desert, as to quality or quantity, but how will penalty, dealt with, properly affect the criminal and others? The possible reformation of the criminal himself and the benefit of others; the protection of the interests of others; the exercise, for these and other reasons, of Divine executive clemency; the mode of doing this so as not to tempt to ill doing, but, rather, to deter from it—all these come in, as helping to some conception of the divinely arranged and accepted atoning mediation. Here, as in the purely judicial view, is justice, righteousness. But it is justice in connection with love, wisdom, infinite compassion—the righteousness of all these attributes in their combined and harmonious co-operation. Our ultimate is not an attribute, but a person—He in whom is all perfection. That Divine person, in the exercise of all these perfections, and with reference to every possible interest, manifests that interest, in the giving of His well-beloved Son to human redemption; in that gift, and as rendering it fully effective, giving Him to a life of human sacrifice, to a death of humiliation and suffering.

But in the light of the New Testament representation, and with the predominant New Testament conception of the Divine relations, God rather as a Sovereign Father than simple Judge or Ruler, we have authority and suggestion, as to what may be called, not the judicial, nor the executive, but the paternal view of the atoning mediation. This includes both of these others, and contains something more. The Heavenly Father, perfect in love to His earthly children, as in His capacity of dealing with them both righteously and lovingly, and with reference to all the possible interests of all, arranges for and accepts the sacrifice and suffering of His well-beloved Son, as a means to the pardon and restoration to favor and life, of His sinful and sin-condemned earthly children; in this, giving and making sacrifice of that Son—"the just for the unjust"—so as to bring them back to life and safety. Here it is not simply justice, as with the judicial view; not simply arrangement and merciful adaptation to the necessities and wants of all, as in the governmental. It is all this, but as going on under the controlling influence of fatherly love, of infinite fatherly interest, and tenderness, and compassion. "God in this commendeth His love toward us." This work of sacrifice and suffering is thus efficacious: first, in the arrangement of Divine justice, love, and wisdom; second, in the character and perfections not only of Him who gave, but of Him who gave Himself, the well-beloved Son; God in Christ working and making sacrifice for man's redemption.

It will thus be seen, as already intimated, that in this is included all that is true in the preceding views of the atoning sacrifice and mediation, and more. It includes the old patristic idea of ransom from the power of Satan. It includes that of example and identification, in feeling and sympathy. It includes that of judicial vindication of Divine righteousness; of Divine administrative righteousness and wisdom. And then, additional to these, pervading them all and giving them a higher significance, that of fatherly love, and interest, and compassion, and self-sacrifice. The love of God, in Christ Jesus our Lord, sparing not His own heavenly Son, but giving Him up for the redemption of His earthly sons, in their sin and condemnation; God, in the person of Christ, sparing not Himself, but giving Himself to the accomplishment of this redemption.

Smeaton's " Doctrine of the Atonement."
J. McLeod Campbell's "Nature of the Atonement."
Cave's " Scripture Doctrine of Sacrifice."
Crawford's " Doctrine of the Atonement."
Martensen's " Dogmatics."
Hill's " Divinity."
See also Knapp's, Hodge's, and Shedd's Theologies.

CHAPTER XVIII.

CHRIST'S WORK IN ITS APPLICATION.

To sinners condemned, justification.—To those morally and spiritually defiled, sanctification.—Relation of these to each other.—To those needing exaltation, heavenly blessedness.—Christ's teaching and example as related to all these.

This work we have looked at, in its different features, as scripturally presented, and as objective to those for whose benefit it takes place. His incarnate life and manifestation; His atoning sacrifice and death; His resurrection and ascension; His intercession—these, in their harmonious co-operation, find their object and result in man's salvation; his deliverance from sin and its evils; his exaltation to heavenly blessedness. The manner and particulars of that operation, subjectively, and as verified in human experience, now demand examination. How are these blessings of Christ's work appropriated?

One of the first of these is that usually described by the word justification. How this comes, is a controverted question. What it is, is no less a point of controversy. The difficulty here, in many cases, has been a mere strife of words. Justification, $\delta\iota\kappa\alpha\iota\acute{o}\sigma\upsilon\nu\eta$, sometimes means righteousness, rightness of disposition; sometimes means rightness of position, acquittal under the Divine law. This last is its meaning in the fifth chapter of Romans. "Being justified, pardoned, and accepted by faith, righted as to our standing and position, we have peace with God." Men as offenders against Divine law, whether sovereignly or fatherly law, need, first of all, pardon, remission, acceptance. This implies removal of the penalty of sins in the past. Justification, therefore, implies this fact: remission of sin and its penalty, acquittal, acceptance under the Divine law. This is for Christ's sake in view of His mediatorial work, especially that of His sufferings and death. In Him, identified with Him, in the act of faith, there is no condemnation. The way in which this is done, we simply allude to for the present. It is the simple truth of remission, of pardon, of acceptance, and acquittal under the Divine law; the change in the earthly subject from the position of a condemned criminal, to that of an accepted and beloved child. "Being justified," "accepted," is the language of the apostle.

Connected with this, and to some degree implied in it, as accomplished in the saving work of Christ, is that already described as sanctification, or rightness of inward disposition; deliverance, release not only from the penalty of sin, but from its power, its bondage. As sin condemns, so it defiles, and enslaves, and debases. Release from, mastery over this, is no less a necessity of human nature; the deliverance of that nature from the evils and consequences of sin, inward as well as outward. As in justification, is the change from the position of the condemned criminal to that of the accepted child, so, in sanctification, there must be one in his inward disposition and character. This last involves the love of holiness in the place of the old love of sin; renewal in the Divine image. The manner of securing this, we do not here examine. We simply note it as a human necessity, for which in Christ's work there is provision.

Usually included in this, and needing to be brought out and distinctly contemplated, is the end, in the purpose and work of Christ; not only that of the pardon of criminals, nor even the full reformation of these criminals, but the full and blessed result to which pardon and reformation are introductory—the salvation, the heavenly exaltation of human nature. Salvation is often used as meaning deliverance from positive evil, outward and inward; but its full meaning goes beyond this. That full meaning may be better expressed by this other word "exaltation," the elevation of human nature to the highest blessedness of which it is capable. In the result of Christ's work is " deliverance from the bondage of corruption," attainment to " the glorious liberty of the sons of God;" positive transformation of the whole man in all his powers and capacities, elevation to a character and condition of heavenly blessedness.

PROVISIONS OF CHRIST'S WORK IN THEIR RECEPTION.

These—justification, sanctification, and heavenly exaltation, as in their nature—have been thus indicated. It remains that we examine the manner in which they become savingly available. These blessings for the race are really efficacious in their reception by individuals. Individuals are justified, are sanctified, are exalted. In the personal reception of these blessings themselves, they become the medium of their communication to others; to them, also, as individuals, and, through them, to a much wider circle. It is thus to this personal reception or appropriation that we now give inquiry. How, first, in order, in this matter, is a man justified? How is it that he obtains forgiveness of sin, Divine favor and forgiveness?

The reply to this question is given in Rom. 5:1, and in the reply to the Philippian jailer: "Being justified by faith, we have," or, as some render it, "let us have peace with God." "Have faith in the Lord Jesus Christ, and thou shalt be saved." Believe is the word here, both in the Authorized and the Revised Version; but it is objectionable as bearing a double sense. The ordinary one, moreover, that in which it is taken by the large majority of readers, is that of mere speculative belief, intellectual assent, acceptance of a fact, upon evidence, or a preponderance of probabilities. The other, that which is meant in these and similar passages, is trust, reliance upon, confidence in a person; the word or character of that person, as in his personality he is known and relied upon. The latter of these is preceded by the former, but does not always accompany it. Intellectual belief of facts, in regard to persons, is a step to faith in them, but does not include it. "Have faith in God," said the Master: "Have faith also in Me;" "Have faith in the Lord Jesus Christ." Such faith, trust, personal confidence, reliance upon the personal Christ, the Son of God in His work and offers, in the word and character of God as revealed in Him, becomes the instrumental means of Divine acceptance and salvation. As God gratuitously offers, so man must gratefully take—not attempt to pay for, or buy, or meritoriously deserve—what is thus offered. "It is of faith," said the apostle, "that it might be by grace. It cannot be by law." It must, therefore, be by grace. If by grace, then through faith. Just as works of obedience and merit are related to law, so is faith to grace. In this act of faith or trust in Christ, and the Divine offers in Him, the soul is justified, has peace. Justification, pardon, acceptance, thus, from its very nature, is no matter of degrees or stages; but is at once accomplished. It is transition from condemnation to pardon, from death to life, from displeasure to favor and acceptance. As it comes by faith, so in the exercise of faith it is accomplished.

But co-instantaneous, as to its incipiency, with justification is sanctification. The blessing of forgiveness, of remission of sin, of acceptance in Christ, is the beginning of an inward change corresponding. The faith which takes Christ's offered blessing, and thus justifies, also and in its very nature begins to sanctify. As men thus live by faith in their justification or escape from death, so they walk by such faith in their subsequent spiritual life. But here, of course, are the elements of degree and progress; the getting rid of the sinful and earthly; the attainment of the spiritually excellent and heavenly. The means and agencies to this are indicated farther on. Just here we direct attention to the nature of the process itself as it goes on—the "cleansing from all filthiness of the flesh and spirit, the perfecting in holiness." The soul, thus, as we have seen, in justification, is put in its proper position, becomes righteous, is righted under the Divine law for its conflict and struggle with evil and sin. In sanctification that struggle inwardly goes on to perfection; thus goes on until death is swallowed up in victory. Sanctification, thus, positively, as well as negatively, is its result. It is holiness, freedom from, and striving against evil; excellence and the striving for its highest attainment. The goal of effort in these respects is the Christ life and character, the Christ approval and blessing.

The result and consequence of these are to be seen in the third particular already mentioned—heavenly exaltation. Justification, freedom from past sin and its curse; sanctification, mastery and freedom from sin and its defilement in the present and future, are thus the divinely arranged steps and stages to something higher—heavenly exaltation. The element of struggle in this last is absent. The conflict has ended in victory. Christ is exalted at the right hand of the Father. Christ's people are partakers of that exaltation. As they have suffered for and with Him, so they reign with Him. It is thus not only deliverance from sin and its consequences, but heavenly elevation and blessedness. In the salvation of Christ all these elements are included.

CHAPTER XIX.

THE BLESSED SPIRIT IN THE WORK OF SALVATION.

Applies and makes efficacious the work of Christ.—This in all its stages.—The spiritual change and transformation, and how described.—His instrumentality.—His personal agency and influence with that instrumentality.

Thus far we have been occupied with the work of the First and Second Persons of the adorable Trinity in human salvation. The Father gives and sends and accepts the mediation of the well-beloved Son. The Son, in His voluntary humiliation, comes, makes sacrifice, and suffers for human deliverance and welfare. The blessed Spirit deals with human nature so as to render the benefits of such work savingly effective. This last we are now called to examine: the quickening and applicative agency and influence of the Spirit, inducing and impelling men, to acceptance and improvement of the divinely provided salvation. He, the Paraclete, the Administrator of Divine truth and Divine influence, thus makes those truths and influences savingly efficacious. His work goes on in all the stages of the redeemed life, already exhibited. Men, for instance, are justified by that faith which is itself a gift of the Spirit, called into existence through His agency, in the presentation of Divine truth. They are sanctified by faith, and love, and all the Divine graces which He, the Spirit, in the exhibition and enforcement of the truth of Christ, calls into existence and nourishes to perfection. And they are eventually glorified and exalted in the exercise of these graces, of which He is the Giver and Dispenser. "God worketh in men." God the Spirit thus personally works in men, in every stage of spiritual life and advancement. As there is need in human nature for Divine spiritual influence, enabling men to appropriate the benefit of Christ's mediation, so that needed influence in the work of the Blessed Spirit is dispensed. If man in this matter works effectually, it is because God the Spirit is working in and with him. The apostles, in their work, have assurance of the presence and power of the Holy Ghost, of the Spirit, the Revealer, the Dispenser and Quickener of Divine truth, as giving effect and success to their undertaking. He, in so doing, would "take of the things of Christ" and reveal to them their full meaning; would "recall to their remembrance" the words of Christ's previous teaching; would "show them things to come," and "lead them into the whole truth" as to His person and work. In so doing with the apostles as their work went on, the Spirit would accomplish certain results with their hearers. He would convict the world of sin; would vindicate the righteousness, and consequently the sufficiency of Christ as a Saviour; would give assurance of the judgment, the condemnation and overthrow of the Evil One, and of all working with him against Christ and His kingdom. This work of the Blessed Spirit, with the preachers and hearers of Divine truth, contemplates in its results, all that is included in the three great stages already indicated. This, His work, not resisted, co-operated with and prayerfully appropriated, the human recipient spirit is justified, sanctified, is finally glorified. It is the Spirit that quickeneth, that giveth life in each and in all these stages, and to their final consummation. In every point of this divinely arranged process, it is the "selfsame Spirit distributing to each one severally as He will."

But while thus generally described, in His sanctifying and saving operation in human nature, there are special forms and modes of expression under which that operation is brought to view. To some of these, therefore, we now give examination. There is the great change from death to life, from the power of Satan to that of God. What are the scriptural aspects under which that change may be contemplated?

The Spiritual Change.

Various words exhibiting the manner of this change are used in Scripture. They may all be regarded as having reference to one great truth—the transition from a state of nature to one of grace; from the condition of earthliness and sin to one of Divine favor and holiness. While to be distinguished logically, as exhibiting aspects of this one fact, they cannot be so chronologically. Most of the confusion on this subject, indeed, has arisen from the effort to make such distinction; as, for instance, between the time of regeneration and renewal, and that, again, of repentance and conversion. We do not scripturally speak of a man as regenerate and unrenewed, or repentant and unconverted. Any one of these implies the others. They are all needed spiritual complements to any one as really accomplished. All these forms of expression help us to understand, in its many-sided significance, this great truth of spiritual experience—that of moral and spiritual change and transformation. In the word "conversion," for instance, turning, $επιστροφη$, is the figure of one going in a wrong or dangerous direction, and turning aside, going back or in another. So, again, "regeneration," $παλινγεννεσία$ and $άναγεννάω$, is that of transition by birth into a new condition; as is $άνακαινωσις$, that of being made over or anew into such conditions. In classical and Jewish usage this word, $παλινγεννεσιά$, expressed the idea of a change to a something better. The manumitted slave, under Roman law, was born again in the process, regenerated. So too with the restored exile, as his sentence of banishment was removed; as was the heathen proselyte born by admission into the covenant blessings of Israel. The word "repentance," $μετανοια$, again, is descriptive of the change of the rational nature; another, $μεταμελεια$, that of the emotional, corresponding. So again there is the figure of men passing from death to life, literally the change from the natural to the spiritual life or condition. In all there is the same truth, but under different representations. Each one contains something not in the others, and yet helping to make those others more intelligible. In the μετανοία, the change as to the νους, the rational, is brought out—this its rational character. In the μεταμελεια, the action of the emotional, of the affections and desires, is indicated. In the επιστροφη is there like implication of that of the volitional; a spiritual change, in which is involved moral action, voluntary determination. And in the παλιγγεννεσία is that of the thorough and complete transformation of the whole character. Some of these, as with παλιγγεννεσια, emphasize the Divine agency to this result. Others, as with επιστροφη, emphasize the human; but in none to the exclusion of that which is in the others. It is a great change and transformation accomplished in the power of the Spirit of God; in the free moral response of the human spirit to His agency and influences. The man thus, in his own moral and spiritual personality, lives the new life. At the same time Christ, by His Spirit, originates this life, and lives in him.

And this brings us into the great topic of the operations of the Blessed Spirit, as related to man's natural condition, and the transformation to the spiritual. This, to some degree, has been implied in what has gone before; but it demands specific consideration. Its importance is that it finds its necessity in the moral and spiritual condition of human nature; its inability, unaided, to appropriate even the provisions and blessings of the salvation of the Gospel. "If any man sin," says one of the apostles, "we have an Advocate, a

Paraclete, a Helper with the Father—Jesus Christ the righteous—and He is the propitiation for our sins." This Advocate or Helper, Jesus, is thus exhibited for the removal of the guilt and penalty of sin. But He who is thus the Helper with reference to this issue, tells of another whose help is directed to another necessity—that of enabling men to know and fully appropriate what He Himself, the propitiating Saviour, had done for them. "I will pray the Father, and He will send you another Helper." "That Helper will lead you into all truth." "He shall testify of Me." In other words, He will fully reveal, and apply, and make efficacious the provision of My salvation. It is a work, first, upon the preachers of the Gospel; taking of the things of Christ and showing them in their full significance; leading them into the whole truth. It is one also upon the hearers, convicting the sinful, pressing that truth upon their minds and consciences, and preparing them for its acceptance.

Looked at collectively, this work of the Spirit, and for both preachers and hearers of the Gospel, is needed; can alone give to that work its divinely intended results and consequences. And, as with men collectively, so with them individually. The preacher, if really what he professes, is himself a transformed man of the Spirit, and his preaching, only under the power of that Spirit, can transform His hearers. The necessity, as already intimated, is in human nature, in its alienation and estrangement from God. "That," says the Master, "which is born of the flesh is flesh." "The carnal mind," says the apostle, "is enmity against God." "We know not what we should pray for as we ought." In these and similar passages is the contrast of the natural and gracious condition. "Those naturally born of the flesh" are graciously born of the Spirit. "The carnal mind, enmity against God," in the reception of the Spirit, becomes "life and peace." Those not knowing how to pray aright, have the Spirit to intercede for, and in them, effectively. The change thus from death to life, from enmity to love, from darkness to light, is wrought in the agency and influences of the Divine Spirit. That change, in some of its stages and results, we have already seen. It remains that we endeavor to ascertain its nature. What, in this change from grace to nature, is involved?

First, we may say there is a change of mind, of the intellectual and rational nature. Through this there will be one upon the emotional nature, the affections and desires; and, through both of these, upon the will. Feeling sometimes goes before reason, and will sometimes anticipate it. But the change, to be thorough and effective, includes all; and in due time each one will have its place. Light, warmth, and energy are needed for this great moral and spiritual change and transformation. In the personality and agency of the blessed Spirit these necessities find their ample provision. That light and warmth and energy are the Divine truths in Christ, ministered by the Spirit of Christ; the Divine truths of Christ's love, and grace, and all-sufficiency for men. These become fully operative, as by His Spirit they are revealed and applied with converting and sanctifying power and energy. The intellect is thus enlightened, affections moved, the will changed and sanctified. "It is," says the Master, "the Spirit that quickeneth." In all these respects to man, dead in trespasses and sins, that Spirit is the quickener, the life-giver.

Just here we encounter the controverted question, as to the nature of this influence, whether or not it is irresistible, and with this the issues of unconditional predestination and final perseverance. As is the first of these questions answered, so logically will be the others. A help to its reply may be found in the instrumentality which the Spirit is described as employing; that instrumentality is Divine truth (1 Pet. 1:22, 23; James 1:18; John 17:17; 15:3; 2 Thess. 2:13; John 8:31, 32; Ps. 19:7, 8; 2 Tim. 3:15, 16, 17). Primarily here the reference is to the truth of Scripture, the divinely inspired word of truth. That truth, however presented, whether in preaching, in sacraments or ordinances, becomes such instrument. The blessed Spirit, using this, is not, however, confined to it in His gracious operations. He may use the truths of nature and of Providence, as He did striving with men before the flood; the truth contained in affliction and blessing; any and every truth, by which men's minds and consciences may be affected. As Divine Spirit, dealing with human spirit, producing a spiritual result, He uses a spiritual instrument to accomplish His purpose. This great change is a moral and spiritual one. From its very nature it demands a moral response on the part of its subject to the Divine influence. As the response of a free moral agent, that response is an act of freedom ; the human spirit yielding to and placing itself at the disposal of the Divine Spirit. God thus beginning, graciously works in man to will and to do. Man, both in willing and in doing, responds to and obeys the Divine impulsion. Salvation in every such instance is of Divine grace—in the blessing offered as in the constraining influence of Him who offers it. And yet it is as Divine grace yielded to and accepted that it becomes savingly operative. If men are predestinated and elected, they are to make their calling and election sure. If they finally persevere, it is as they perseveringly respond to the aids and influences of the Divine Helper and Sanctifier. They are always dealt with as able to act otherwise ; to resist the Divine influences, and thus fail as to their final benefit. There is thus election to advantages and privileges. As this is responded to, the full result is the election of blessing. The former is unconditional, the latter conditional. And in both, the elect are made so, not to enjoy these privileges and blessings alone and only for themselves, but to extend and communicate them to others.

One other point needs to be brought out clearly and distinctly. The Spirit, it has been said, uses the truth as an instrument. Is not that truth all with which we have to do ? In other words, is not the whole work of the Blessed Spirit in this matter to reveal these truths as they are given to us in the inspired Word; and in giving us that, has He not entirely fulfilled His commission? Manifestly this does not meet the scriptural declarations on this subject. The Spirit does indeed reveal the truth. But He also uses it. He is present dealing with the human spirit in such usage. "Neither He that planteth, nor He that watereth, but God giveth the increase." Here the apostle is speaking of truth thus used in spiritual planting, but needing divinely quickening power. So too, when he speaks of God working in them, to will and to do, the same idea is implied. The peculiarity, indeed, of the Spirit's work to abide with men forever, in this view, is disposed of. He would thus turn over His work to the written word. Men are now living under the dispensation of the Spirit. One of the pervading truths of that dispensation, is this of His presence and power; His presence and power in all moral and spiritual agencies; His influence and agency through these, and with these upon spiritual agents, urging them and aiding them in the way of life. Christ bodily absent is present by His Spirit, to His Church and people, in their work and spiritual life, even to the end of the world.

CHAPTER XX.

THE CHURCH AND SACRAMENTS.

The Church invisible and visible, ideal and actual.—Teaching of the Articles.—Sacraments ordained of Christ.—How different from other sacred ordinances.—Baptism and its effects.—Question as to its form, its subjects, by whom administered.—The Lord's Supper.—The two questions of difference and controversy.—Sacrificial character.—That of the kind of presence.

THE bringing in, by the Blessed Spirit, of individuals to the reception of Christ and the benefits of His work of salvation, is the transition inwardly from the state of nature to that of grace, externally from the world to the Church. This last is the community of the redeemed. Identification with Christ inwardly by a spirit of grateful devotion and loyal obedience, outwardly by baptismal profession, is demanded of each one of His followers. Thus associated in His name, they are to do His work, to bring men under His dominion—in other words, they are to enlarge the Church or discipleship until it includes the race, all nations. It is a visible institution rooted in invisible and spiritual realities. And it looks forward in its results to the spiritual conquest of the world.

The XIX. Article, as those that follow, is occupied with this visible Church. Its notes or features are profession of Christ, the preaching of the pure

Word of God, sacraments duly administered, errancy in doctrine of some of the most eminent of the early churches, as also that of Rome. Its authority, in this respect, while affirmed in Articles XX. and XXXIV., is, at the same time, limited by that of Scripture; the same implication being contained in the XXI. Article of the English Church on General Councils. A ministry is contemplated in Article XXIII., the necessity of a lawful call and sending, by the duly authorized men for that purpose, and in Article XXXVI. the Episcopal consecrations and ordinations of the book of Edward VI. are accepted as free from superstition, and to be used in the English Church. But there is no affirmation as to its exclusive effect, or as to its bearing upon the validity of orders received elsewhere. The men who drew up these articles, as a matter of historic fact, accepted these orders—Roman, Lutheran, and Reformed—and with the two latter had communion.

The distinction is frequently made of the Church visible and invisible. Dean Field uses these terms. Hooker uses the word mystical for invisible; but in his discussion it comes to the same thing. The object in this distinction seems to have been to affirm the real church-membership of individuals and communities, expelled by persecution or otherwise from the visible church,—those without organization, or with but an imperfect one. The idea was the real, mystic, invisible, spiritual connection with Christ, of all His real, believing people, not destroyed by anything of a mere outward character. Visibly cut off, invisibly they were living in Him. The visible Church would thus be the aggregate of all visible communities, constituting one outward whole. The invisible would be the aggregate of all individuals, of all genuine Christians, those in the visible Church, as those, if any, outside. The purposes of this distinction, while expressing an important truth, have largely passed away.

Another mode of looking at this subject would be under the aspects of the Church ideal and the Church actual. Without the use of these terms, we find the facts which they imply in the New Testament. There is, in the epistles, at times, to the contemplation of the apostles, a glorious Church, as yet unrealized—the "spotless bride of Christ," without defect or excrescence; the Church, what it ought to be inwardly and outwardly. At the same time they speak, and legislate for, and give direction to actual churches. Some of these are defective in doctrine; others seem to be only partially organized as to their ministry; and others with moral defects among their membership. As associated in the profession by baptism, of Christian fellowship, they are all spoken of and treated as churches. So is it now. The ideal is not as yet actualized. The actuals, even the best, fall far short of it. Some imagine that they are, in outward organism. But beyond that, the claim has not been ventured. A clear view of what that ideal involves and demands, and the earnest effort to its attainment, outwardly and inwardly, would be one of the death blows to unloving sectarianism. The great and proper work, for each one of these forms of the actual, is to be striving and making effort for the Divine ideal.

Christian Sacraments.

This word "sacrament," in connection with Christianity, first occurs in a heathen writer. Pliny, in his letter to Trajan, speaks of the Christians as binding themselves by a sacramentum, or pledge, to certain actions or courses. Whether, in any way, it was thus associated with the reception of the Lord's Supper, it is impossible, from the connection, to determine. As the supper was usually a part of the Christian services, it may have been that part of it to which this expression had reference. Both in this and in the other sacrament—baptism—there is involved one of the elements of the sacramentum—the military oath by which the soldier bound himself to a course of fidelity to his leader. Converts from the world were baptized, sacramented, pledged to a loyal discipleship. Disciples in the supper, so to speak, renewed their sacrament, reminded themselves and others of their assumed obligations to the redeeming Master, and in Him to each other. Both originally instituted by the Master, rested upon His supreme authority. Whatever may be said of other institutions of an edifying or appropriate character, as related to certain acts of religious service, those say of confirmation or ordination, their ground of acceptance and usage is simply their adaptation to the ends proposed. They want the element present in baptism and the Lord's Supper, of specific Divine institution. The essentials of a Christian sacrament, not only in the judgment of Protestant theologians, but even in that of the Council of Trent, must include this, its Divine institution. Having a form of words and some material element to which they are related, they become authoritative as divinely appointed.

Sacrament of Baptism.

Baptism, as the initiative pledge of Christian discipleship, rests, of course, upon the specific institution (Matt. 28: 19; Mark 16: 15, 16) of the Master. The interpretation of the command thus given is afforded in the record of apostolic action during the next thirty years following. Such baptism pledges to faith in Him and devotion to Him, as fully manifested, not only in His teaching, but in His atoning work, His attesting resurrection and triumphant ascension: as the Son of Man, the Son of God; and thus, with the Father and the Holy Ghost, in the Trinity of the Divine Unity.

Baptisms prior to this were, so to speak, of an introductory character. Their earliest forms were in the symbolic washings of the Levitical system. Later was the proselyte baptism of heathen converts, preceding the circumcision, by which they were admitted to the privileges of Judaism. John's baptism, later on, was connected with the announcement of the Messiah and His kingdom, and to the higher baptism that Messiah Himself would administer. Still later was the baptism by our Lord's disciples (compare John. 3 : 22 ; 4 : 2), in connection with His actual manifestation. No intimation is afforded as to the baptism of the apostles themselves. Some of them, as disciples of John, had received his baptism.* That of the Holy Ghost and with fire, fitted them to administer that of water to others.

As to its usage, as already intimated, it begins on the day of Pentecost, and we find it in connection with converts as subsequently made. Doubt has been suggested as to whether the formula (Matt. 28 : 19) was always used. It is not specifically mentioned; in some cases, too, persons are spoken of as baptized in the name of the Lord Jesus. Both of these facts, however, are perfectly consistent with its usage. The natural probability is heavily against its non-usage. As, moreover, it continued in the ages following in such usages, and the apostles, and other creeds really seem to be this formula, expanded for catechetical instruction, preceding baptism, we may regard the rite and its form of words as perpetuated through the subsequent ages of Christianity until the present. No one anticipates that a change in this respect is now possible.

Two points have arisen as to its administration of a controversial character.

One of these is as to its manner, whether by immersion, pouring, or sprinkling, and as to whether the original manner, if undoubted, is essential to the sacrament, and, of course, to Christian discipleship. The main issue is as to the last. Many who think immer-

---

* See Robert Hall's discussion as to the bearing of this upon close communion, vol. i., p. 304.

sion probably the original form, do not regard it as essential, the great truth symbolized in all these modes being this essential. Others regard it as both the original form, and the only valid one. Under something like the distinction of the visible and invisible Church, these last recognize the distinction of baptized and unbaptized Christian believers.

So, too, as to the subjects of baptism. Some affirm that it is only for adults, capable of assuming its obligations; others, and the great majority of Christendom, admitting the child upon the faith and pledges of the Christian parent, look forward in due time to his own assumption of them. This is in the line of Divine dealing, under the old dispensations, patriarchal and Mosaic; and peculiarly in sympathy with the spirit and declaration of the Master Himself as to little children.

One other point needs to be noted—the proper administrator. Ordinarily it has been held, the persons appointed by the Church for this duty. The apostles, if they themselves baptized, seem, in some cases, to have turned it over to subordinate officers. And St. Paul speaks of the infrequency of his own personal baptizing. At certain periods, lay persons, by Church appointment, largely administered the sacrament. The principle seems to have been accepted that the administrator might be of the order, but not necessarily of the essence, of the sacrament. Baptism, in decorous form, with water, in the name of the adorable Trinity, it was ruled, ought not to be repeated. If doubt as to any of these, then repetition or hypothetical form of administration. Passing from these to the more prominent question of the effects of the sacrament, we may take the various points enumerated in the XXVII. Article. First, as to adults.

(*a*) Baptism is a sign of profession and mark of difference between Christians and non-Christians.

(*b*) Baptism, rightly received, is a sign of regeneration or new birth; is an instrument of grafting into the Church; is a visible signing and sealing of the Divine promises of forgiveness of sin and of Divine adoption.

(*c*) Baptism thus rightly received, confirms faith and increases grace.

The statement *a*, it will be seen, is unconditional. It is the ecclesiastical *opus operatum* of all baptized in due form.

But *b* and *c* are conditional. In other words, there is the transition from the actual baptism of *a* to the ideal of *b* and *c*; from the baptism that may be in any particular case, to that which ought to be in all. Evidently the real spiritual blessing of baptism here, is not in the objective sacrament alone, but in the subjective recipiency of the person baptized. As in the article on the Lord's Supper, the reception of the spiritual blessing is made to depend upon its faithful, its believing reception.

But, then, it is asked, does the validity of the sacrament depend upon the subjective condition of the recipient? Not at all. This is to confound two things that in themselves are distinct. The sacrament, properly administered, in this, has its ecclesiastical validity. Supposing its recipient, coming to a cognizance of the fact, six months or twenty years afterward, that he had received it in a worldly or unbelieving spirit, he would not need to be baptized again. That ecclesiastical, outer part is done. And he, now seeing what it means and demands, must endeavor to meet its obligations. Ordinances do not depend for their validity upon inward states. If so, they could never be certified; but the inward, personal experiences of their benefits do. The inward blessing of the sacrament is, in all cases, as is the faith of him who participates in it.

The same principle also applies to the long-contested and complicated issue of the spiritual regeneration, associated with infant baptism. Here, as in the adult, is the actual and the ideal baptism. In some particular actual, the outward rite is duly administered; but the parents and sponsors are thorough worldlings, and the conditions of the after-faith of the child, and that after-faith itself, have no existence. In such case there is ecclesiastical regeneration. In another particular actual, is also the ideal. The child is prayerfully and believingly consecrated; and his response of faith as he comes to the capacity for its exercise, secures the blessing. Here is the spiritual as well as the ecclesiastical regeneration. The service, in its terms, assumes that it is the ideal in all cases, and predicates the result. But that result, as with the adult, is conditional. If the baptism is what it ought to be, so the blessing; if not, otherwise.

The Sacrament of the Lord's Supper.

The sacrament of the supper, having its special reference to Christ's sacrificial work, as does that of baptism to the transforming agency of the Blessed Spirit, in point of time, as to its institution, preceded that of baptism. It was to the twelve, not to the whole discipleship, on the night preceding the crucifixion. That it was intended for all, comes out later in apostolic practice; the apostles, in its first institution, representing the whole body of the discipleship. The breaking of bread in the Acts of the Apostles, and the allusions to it in the epistles, as also the later practice of the early Church, show its observance; and there can be no reasonable doubt of its continuance until the present time. Modifications as to its meaning and efficacy, and the manner of its reception and benefit, have come in during the intervening periods. But, whatever the character of these, whether regarded as a sacrifice or the memorial of a sacrifice, whether as a symbolic representation of Christ's body, or Christ's body substantially or materially present, its observance continues unbroken. In some of these forms or other, the effort is made to show forth "Christ's death until He come." We may say, with little doubt or hesitation, that wherever and so long as Christianity lasts, this sacrament will be continued in its observance.

Two deeply interesting issues present themselves in connection with this sacrament. The first has reference to its sacramental nature; the second, to the manner of its efficacy. The reply to the first to some degree anticipates the second. They may, however, for clearness be distinguished.

First, then, is the Lord's Supper a sacrifice? Is such sacrifice that of the cross repeated, or one made on the night of the supper?* If so, there is nothing of it in the language of the institution. "Take, eat, this is My body," is the language of the Master; "drink ye all of it; for this is My blood of the New Testament, which is shed for many for the remission of sins" (Matt. 26: 26, 28; Mark 14: 22, 24; Luke 22: 19, 20). "The cup of blessing," says the apostle, "which we bless, is it not the communion, the common participation," of the blood of Christ? The bread which we break, is it not the "communion of the body of Christ"? "The Lord Jesus took bread, and when He had given thanks, He brake it, and said, Take, eat; this is My body, which is broken for you; do this in remembrance of Me." "This cup is the New Testament in My blood;" "this do, as oft as ye drink it, in remembrance of Me." "Ye do show forth the Lord's death." (See 1 Cor. 10: 16, 17; 11: 23, 24.) These are the inspired accounts of the institution, and its significance. In none of them is there allusion to its sacrificial character. "Christ," says the apostle, "our Passover, is sacrificed for us." But here, again, there is no allusion to any such sacrifice anticipated or re-

* These need to be distinguished. They are so in the doctrine of the mass.

peated in the Lord's Supper. The idea is unscriptural; in the light of the Epistle to the Hebrews, anti-scriptural. The one Priest and the one Sacrifice, in their perfection and finality, exclude the possibility of any other or others. Just as the old Jewish and heathen conception, that a minister of religion must be a sacrificing priest, worked its way into the declining Christianity of the third and fourth century, so did this of the Lord's Supper as a re-enacted sacrifice: sometimes as the sacrifice on the cross repeated; sometimes, as in the Trentine doctrine of the mass, the repetition either of that on the cross, or of one offered on the night of the institution of the supper.

But may it not, it has been asked—may it not be called a memorial sacrifice? In some of the secondary senses of the word sacrifice, and as descriptive of the state of mind of the recipients, doubtless such forms of expression may be used. They are very apt, eventually, to lead astray. Much safer and more scriptural is the language of the Church Catechism—"a remembrance of the sacrifice of the death of Christ, and of the benefits which we receive thereby;" not "a memorial sacrifice," but "a memorial of a sacrifice." So also the XXVIII. Article calls it "a sacrament," a pledged assurance "of our redemption by Christ's death." Just as baptism, a divinely covenanted sacramentum, oath, or pledge of the regenerative grace of the Blessed Spirit to those in faith seeking it, so is the supper of the redemptive efficacy of Christ's work, to those in like faith relying upon it for salvation.

Often identified with this last, but really of very different significance, is "the sacrifice of thanksgiving," to which allusion is made in the communion service. Here the sacrifice is not one of the sacramental elements, but of the persons thankfully receiving them. It is the great body of the spiritual priesthood, in grateful remembrance of the sacrifice of Christ, thankfully offering themselves to Him and His service in return. This is the spiritual sacrifice pertaining to the whole redeemed life, but here solemnly recognized in its obligatory character and gratefully reaffirmed : "The sacrifice of praise to God, the fruit of lives, our earnest devotion and grateful service."

Connected with this question of the sacrifice, in the sacrament of the supper, is that of the presence. This word presence, which has given so much trouble, does not occur in our communion service, in our Articles or Catechism, or in Scripture. In some of their expressions, however, this issue is implicated.

The great difficulty, in this matter, is the ambiguity of many of the terms employed. Some, however, are undoubted as to their single meaning. There is, for instance, the affirmation of (*a*) the transubstantiated presence ; (*b*) the consubstantiated presence ; (*c*) the substantiated presence ; (*d*) the representative or symbolic presence.

All these are objective to the recipient, and whatever his moral and spiritual condition. In the first three, Christ's body is corporally present in the elements. In the third, it is so symbolically and representatively.

But there are other forms of expression descriptive of this presence, full of ambiguity.

"Real presence" mostly, for the first century after the Reformation, the equivalent of "corporal," "transubstantiated." Sometimes, now, in the same sense; sometimes as opposed to fictitious or imaginary. With some, again, the equivalent of spiritual; with others, some kind of corporal.

"Spiritual presence." This is usually the equivalent of Christ's presence in the elements to the faith of the recipient; the suffering Christ in His sacrifice present to those appropriating the benefit of that sacrifice; and with this, the presence of the glorified Christ, ministered by His Spirit to His believing people, and thus fulfilling His promise of being with them, when assembled in His name. Faith, it may be said, combines these aspects of the absent Saviour, and brings Him to loving contemplation and communion.

"Sacramental presence" is a term of more recent usage. It may mean any of the others. Recently it is a form in which transubstantiation, or some of its modifications, is asserted. All forms of such presence are, of course, in some sense sacramental.

"Substantial presence." The effort in this seems to be to affirm the fact of the real bodily presence, without attempting to describe its mode, as is done in the terms trans and consubstantiation. As, however, under substantial it affirms corporal, it has all the difficulties of both of these: body, that which in its very definition is outlined, without outline, ubiquitous.

Amid all these diversities of statement and apparent difference of view, it may be said that they are but variations of two, under which they may all be comprehended: the spiritual and the corporal. In the first is the presence of Christ's body and blood, objective, symbolized, represented in the elements; the presence subjective of the personal Christ, ministered by His Spirit, to the spirit, the mind and heart of His faithful disciple. In the second is the presence of Christ's body and blood objective, corporally transubstantiated, consubstantiated, or substantiated in the elements; there is the subjective presence it may be to faith, but also certainly to the bodily organs of those receiving, containing, and conveying the grace which it signifies, when that grace is not positively resisted. These are the two systems. Many of the expressions noted are intended to avoid either; to find a *tertium quid*, and thus keep clear of what are regarded extremes of both. In some cases, too, theological and ecclesiastical experts manage to keep up the appearance of such mediate position. But their unsophisticated pupils are more consistent. The teacher, in many cases, is able to halt in the middle of a syllogism. But the pupil, in his simplicity, goes on to the conclusion. Calvin and the English Reformers, in their effort to find a harmonizing statement for the Lutherans and Zwinglians, were not always perfectly consistent. Such inconsistency, however, does not appear in the Articles and standards.

While the diversity and strife of this subject has

been one of the reproaches of Christendom, it may, at the same time, be urged, and truthfully, that it indicates the deep interest as to all particulars of the Christian Church in this solemn ordinance of the Master's appointment, as in the great event which it was intended to commemorate.

Article XXXI. denies in the most emphatic manner the sacrificial nature of the supper, and, of course, the doctrine of the mass. Article XXVIII. condemns transubstantiation. While it does not use the word "presence," it affirms that the body of Christ, represented in the bread, is given, taken, and received only after a heavenly and spiritual manner; and that faith is the medium or means of reception. If any kind of presence be thus implied, "spiritual" would best express it. Of course the only kind of presence in dispute is that of Christ's body, His human nature. In His Divine nature He is, of course, Omnipresent. The difficulty with most of the affirmations of bodily presence is that of ubiquity, really monophysitism.

The further question has been raised as to which body of our Blessed Lord—that of the humiliation or that of the exaltation—is present in any of these forms in the supper. Strictly speaking, there is no which in this matter. The $ἴδιον\ σῶμα$, "the identical body" of our Lord, as of that of His people, is the same in its exaltation, as in its humiliation. Manifestly, however, the body represented in the broken bread and the poured-out wine, is that which suffered on the cross, seen by faith as thus represented. That same faith, however, sees that same body now exalted at the right hand of the Father. But more living, and closer still, to that faith, is the living, personal Christ, according to His promise, and by His Spirit revealed as present to His believing disciple.

With these two questions of the sacrificial character of the Lord's Supper, and the manner of His presence, is that of its sacramental benefit or efficacy. These, as noted in Articles XXV. and XXVIII., are twofold: those of an ecclesiastical, and those of a moral and spiritual character. The former are invariable, the latter variable. The outward sacrament, duly administered, includes the former *ex opere operato;* the latter come only in the proper inward reception. The supper of the Lord, for instance, is ecclesiastically:

(*a*) Invariably a sign or symbol of the love which Christians ought to have to each other.

(*b*) Invariably an outward sacrament or pledge of our redemption by Christ's death.

(*c*) Morally and variably, a participation of Christ's body and blood—those rightly, worthily, and with faith receiving, thus participating; others not. Such participation of the faithful, not physical, but in a heavenly and spiritual manner, by faith.

The sacrament in such case is a valid, ecclesiastical transaction to all. Some who partake, receive its full blessing. Others fail so to do. The presence or absence of faith constitutes the ground of difference as to results. These results, objective and ecclesiastical, are invariably in the ordinance duly administered. The subjective spiritual benefit is variably conditioned upon the subjective state of the recipient.

CHAPTER XXI.

ANGELOLOGY.

Angelic existence.—Early intimations.—Manifestations of presence and agency in Old Testament Names of Angels, and degrees.—Manifestations in New Testament.—Fallen Angels.—Their Leader.—Demoniacal possessions.

THEOLOGY, the doctrine of God, and anthropology, the doctrine of man, have their immediate and practical interest, and as related to all times and possible circumstances. Angelology, the doctrine of other beings or intelligences, related to God in one direction, to man in another, so far as revealed, properly claims attention. No specific account as to their creation is given. "As sons of God" (Job 38 : 7) they are spoken of as rejoicing in the creation of our world; and in Col. 1 : 16, as among things invisible, they themselves are elsewhere spoken of as created. This name, "angel," describes their peculiar characteristic, as in connection with our world, sent ones, or messengers. "Ministering spirits," says the apostle, "sent forth to minister to those who shall be heirs of salvation (Heb. 1 : 14). Their relations Godward and manward are thus exhibited. Such statements may not be intended to be exhaustive. So far as regards one class of men, it brings to view their predominent work; as, under this, others may be included. It is one of which there are many scriptural illustrations, and strikingly describes their agency in human affairs. The truth of the existence of such beings, however in accordance with what might be anticipated, from the immensity and manifoldness of creation, is here grounded upon the fact of its specific revelation. The ultimate question is as to the satisfactory evidence of such revelation.

That revelation begins at a very early period. The cherubim, keeping the way of the tree of life, living beings of some form or other, have been regarded as the first. As these, however, in later Scripture seem to be rather symbolic exhibitions of Divine or natural powers than personal agents, so they may be here. The earlier manifestations to the patriarchs were theophanies. But with these, beginning with Abraham, were the angelic. The same were made to Hagar and Jacob. And in the deliverance from Egypt, their presence and agency is more than once to be recognized. The law, indeed, is spoken of "as a dispensation of angels," "as ordained of angels." And in the Psalms their presence is alluded to in connection with its promulgation; as, in its subsequent administration in the history of the chosen people, we are frequently told of their interpositions. Sometimes, indeed, the powers of nature, winds and storms, are personified as Divine angels or messengers. Sometimes, again, the expression, "Sons of God," applicable to angels, is applied to good men. But the connection usually makes clear what is intended. While winds and storms are

God's messengers, and good men are His sons, yet, besides these, He has His angelic sons and His personal angelic messengers of heavenly power and intelligence. Throughout the Old Testament the existence and work of these personal angelic beings are exhibited. Toward its close we find specific names—"Michael," "who as God," and "Gabriel," "man of God"—given to two of them. Whether the former of these, as the angel Jehovah of Genesis, was not a manifestation of the Divine Logos in the Old Testament, has been made a question. We find in the New Testament one of them spoken of as an archangel, and the other as standing in the presence of God. So, again, the trump of the archangel is spoken of in connection with the resurrection. But no specific account beyond the fact of preeminence is given as to what in this appellation is fully implied.

Coming more particularly to the New Testament, we find these manifestations of angelic agency and interest in the heirs of salvation. They herald the coming of the Christ, the promised Deliverer; warn of impending dangers to Him in His infancy; minister to Him after His trial in the wilderness. One is with Him in Gethsemane. Others are at the tomb on the morning of the resurrection. And at His ascension two of them give assurance of His visible return to His disciples and people. So, too, in His own teaching, angels of little children are spoken of as beholding the face of His Father in heaven. The beggar Lazarus is borne of angels to Abraham's bosom. Angels are spoken of as coming with the Son of Man in His glory. And more than twelve legions of them are spoken of as at His call, in the arrest in Gethsemane. Angelic presence and agency are thus clearly manifested. The same agency comes to view in the record of apostolic effort and labor. And, in the last book of Scripture, we find this agency on earth as in heaven in the great conflict, which finally terminates in the triumph of righteousness. "Michael and his angels" are on one side, the dragon and his angels on the other. In this conflict there are also the beast and the false prophet, representing classes of men opposing Christ, and the saints for Him. At the same time, with these human agents, and doing their part in the conflict, are these angelic ones: good and bad men, Michael and his angels, and the dragon and his angels.

In reference to all the manifestations thus far of angelic existence and agency, with one exception it is that of beings habitually and spontaneously moving under the impulse or conformity to the Divine will: "Sons of God," "Bene Elohim," as in the filial spirit of loving obedience that Divine will controls and regulates all their movements. They have thus kept their high estate; passed safely through their original probation, attaining the security of habitual and heavenly excellence.

Contrasted with these are other angelic beings of a different character: fallen angels, not keeping their high estate; miserable in their fall, and hostile to God, as also to His earthly subjects and creatures.

ANGELOLOGY. 241

Just as the good angels, in their love and obedience to God, are described as endeavoring to bless and benefit His creature, man, so the fallen, as opposing His will and endeavoring to injure and destroy His earthly creatures. Distinction must here be made as to the term evil angels, especially as sometimes used in the Old Testament. This may mean natural agencies of calamity, as the pestilence, the storm, the famine. It may, again, mean angels obedient to God, the instruments of His judgments of disaster; as when sent to execute such judgment upon Sodom or upon Pharaoh and the Egyptians. Distinct from these are angelic beings morally evil in character, the fallen ones to whom allusion has already been made. Their existence comes to view especially in the New Testament. Their leader and prince, Satan, or the devil, is described, in the teaching of Jesus and the apostles, as exercising his powers of enticement and temptation upon men; as opposing the Divine will, and working in men to disobedience and transgression. And intimations are given as to his malignant work in the first temptation of man, "the murderer and liar from the beginning;" later, in the trial of Job, as in the evil influence exerted upon Saul. With him, also, as his followers, are other evil spirits, and working to the same malignant and mischievous purposes. As the work of Christ was to destroy those of the devil, to overthrow his kingdom, so in the New Testament, the existence and agency of Satan and his angels are more fully brought out and exhibited. The conflict, in its various forms and stages as it goes on, is more fully brought to view in the Apocalypse; and its final result is seen in their complete and perfect overthrow. All enemies are to be put under Christ's feet. This includes not only all opposing human agency, but that which is Satanic and diabolical.

Having its connection with this subject is the very difficult one of demoniacal possession. One mode of getting rid of this difficulty is to identify these possessions with cases of ordinary insanity. Doubtless in some of the cases, phenomena of insanity are exhibited. Perhaps insanity was one of its usual accompaniments. In one case a father, bringing his son to our Lord, speaks of him as a lunatic; and yet, in the same connection, he is spoken of as under demoniacal agency. It has thus been argued that, as our Blessed Lord spoke in the forms of expression then in current usage, and as He did not stop to explain that the lunatic, Σεληνιαζομενος, was not moon-struck, so with the Δαιμωνιαζεμενος, the supposed demon-struck. And if the mere names in these cases were all, this explanation might be satisfactory. There are, however, other accompaniments which seem to present to it insuperable difficulty. Our Lord not only spoke of the demons, but to them, and commanded their departure. The demons knew Him and His authority. His parable of the unclean spirit going out of a man and seeking rest, and finding none, and of his re-entrance with others worse into the empty habitation, and His language in reply to the charge of casting out demons by

Satanic assistance—all show that we are beyond the region of mere insanity. It is a revelation of the spirit world, unique and peculiar. And, as such, however mysterious, and as only mysterious, must be accepted.

The only question, in such case, is, Are there analogous facts natural, so that the mystery does not involve contradiction? Regarding the demoniac as accountable—accountable for being in such state, and thus, to some degree, for his actions in such state—the analogous cases are around us in abundance. The demon of strong·drink, of opium, of licentious indulgence, often produces a condition as wretched and irrational as that of the demonized in the New Testament. If this, their condition, was thus the result of some habit of previous indulgence, the mystery of an evil spirit coming in and taking possession of such a man remains; but the moral difficulty disappears. It is the act of the man, under Divine permission and arrangement, bringing its results in this form.

So, too, if we suppose the demon possessed not accountable for his condition, or as in a condition in which his accountability has passed away. Analogous cases we find all around, in the phenomena of ordinary insanity and other diseases, under the operation of the law of heredity. Insanity is something with which we are familiar, and we imagine we know something about it. But its problems, its moral problems, who will undertake to solve? Prior to experience, how violently improbable that rational beings, men, too, of the highest order of intellect, could come into such condition? On the other hand, how much like the demonized, the self-made victim of vicious habit and indulgence? How often similar result seen in the innocent inheritors of their vicious constitutions? Men, again, brutalize themselves, and they come into the condition and even the diseases and habits of the brute creation. We are fearfully and wonderfully made. And while there is moral safety to the upright, the result of its opposite, and in all directions, is incalculable. The demoniacal possession, a great supernatural mystery, has its many natural analogies. Specially manifested during the ministry of Him whose mission was to destroy the works of the devil, still, even as belonging to that special dispensation of the past, it has its present lessons of profitable suggestion.

CHAPTER XXII.

ESCHATOLOGY.

Its particulars matter of pure revelation.—The final transition.—Resurrection, Judgment.—The two great classes.

The knowledge thus spoken of, in one sense a knowledge of the end, in another is a knowledge of that which is without end, the world of endless realities. Even as related to the events closing the present condition of things, the end of earthly existence, with its relations, such knowledge is dependent upon specific revelation. As, in such knowledge, we pass into the region of the supernatural, so it is only in a supernatural way, and by supernatural agencies, that we can come to its attainment. "In the Gospel," says the apostle, "Jesus Christ hath brought to light life and immortality." To some of the main points of this revelation, completive of all that had gone before, we now give our examination.

In so doing we naturally think of what may be called the divinely indicated transition, from man's present to his future state of being. Prior even to this, however, is the deeply interesting truth of the nature of such transition—from mortality to immortality, from temporal to eternal existence. "God," says one of the apocryphal writers, "created man in the image of His own immortality." This is the constant implication of Scripture, especially of the New Testament Scripture. Dying creatures, as to this world, men are undying in the world to which they are going. It is, therefore, the transition from a temporal to an eternal existence.

Two facts involved in that transition come prominently to view—the resurrection and final judgment. The first of these—the resurrection—going back, in its assurance, to the resurrection of Christ, and looking forward in its anticipation, to the fulfilment of His declarations. As also to the exercise of His Divine power, it brings out and emphasizes the deeply interesting truth of the continuance of the whole man, bodily as well as spiritual, beyond this present state, and into that which is beyond. As there is a natural body, a body adapted to the conditions of the present animal organism, so there is a spiritual body, adapted to the conditions of spiritual existence. The body thus, in its two stages or conditions, is treated and spoken of as the same, changed and changeable, but not losing its identity, in these its different stages of existence and of action. As it was with the Master in these respects, so with His disciples. He the firstfruits, in His resurrection ; His people, in the morning of the resurrection, the fully ripened and gathered harvest. At the same time, while emphasizing this fact of the resurrection of Christ's people, the truth is also exhibited of that of the whole race, "of the just and of the unjust" (Acts 24 : 15 ; John 5 : 28, 29 ; 1 Cor. 15 ; 1 Thess. 4 : 13, 18).

Closely associated in Divine teaching with this truth of the general resurrection, is that of the judgment. The two classes arise, the one to a resurrection of life, the other to one of condemnation. While there may be difficulty in forming conceptions of this judgment, its outward circumstances and manifestations, the truth of its reality, in the light of Scripture, is clear and undoubted. While each one shall give an account of himself, the implication is that it will be in connection with others ; if not the whole world of human beings literally, at least that world of human beings to which the individual was related ; which affected him, and which he affected in his individual life and course of action. "Every one," says the apostle, "shall give an account of himself to God" (Rom. 14 : 12). "We must all appear before the judgment-seat of Christ" (2 Cor. 5 : 10). "Before the Son of Man shall be gathered all nations" (Matt. 25 : 31, 32). "I saw the dead, small and great, stand before God" (Rev. 20 : 12).

And these two events—resurrection and judgment—as already intimated, are the transition to the life beyond this world. That existence—certainly in the New Testament conception, whatever may be the questions and difficulties as to the teaching of the Old Testament—is an endless one. Created in the image of God, renewed in the image of Christ, the Son of God, man becomes partaker of Divine, endless existence.

Eternal life is the portion of Christ's redeemed people. This life, in its fulness and blessedness, is not exhausted as to its meaning in the words "endless existence." It is that, and much more. "They shall not die forever," is one declaration of the Master. "They shall have eternal life," is another. The latter includes the former, and goes far beyond and above it. It is endless rest, deliverance for all that is evil, and in all its forms. It is endless life, elevation to all the blessedness of which man is capable: "the new heavens and the new earth, wherein dwell righteousness;" the redeemed "creation," delivered out of the bondage of corruption, translated "into the glorious liberty of the sons of God." God created man in His own Divine image. In the person of His well-beloved Son He assumed man's human image, that He might make him like Himself, holy, happy, blessed, in the full, and perfect, and joyous exercise of all His divinely given powers and capacities.

The mournful contrast to this demands contemplation; the condition of the unsaved, the effect of persevering impenitence. The judgment introduces them into a world of condemnation; and the prospect is of continuance. No prospect is held up of relief or remission. The sentence in each case is a just one, in perfect accordance with desert, and as related to all kinds and degrees of evil character. What will be the effect of such penalty, and the conditions which it will involve, no specific information is given. In view of the fearful truth of such penalty, and its possibilities, various replies have been ventured. One, for a long time prevalent, and especially of a popular preaching and conception, was that it will make its subjects morally worse and more malignant; and, as the effect of that, more miserable and wretched. The recoil from this was universalism—sin really punished in this world, and the race saved by the redeeming work for another. A modification of this was that of restorationism; this after the administration of due penalty and reformation. Still another of this was the theory of conditional immortality; such immortality to those reformed and purified under this penalty, annihilation to those under it failing so to do. And still another: that of annihilation to all, either at once or after a time of retribution. The difficulty with all, after the first, is that they bring to an end what is represented without termination. And, that of the first, is its conflict with the perfections of the Divine character. Divine penalty is thus made purely and only productive of misery and suffering. The same course alluded to, in connection with explanations of the doctrine of the atonement, has been pursued here—that of looking at only one attribute of Divine perfection. Strict justice, perfect righteousness, is the attribute present in such penalty. Is it the only one? Can this be affirmed? God is just; but He is also wise and loving. Even in His strange work of inflicting punishment He does not and cannot deny Himself, divest Himself of any of His perfections. While He cannot look upon iniquity but with abhorrence, He cannot look upon suffering but with interest and compassion. With the justice that chastens and punishes is the love, the compassion over its objects, and the necessity of its exercise. "If I make my bed in hell, Thou art there also." He is there in justice; but also in compassion, in the interest of love over the suffering even of the evil-doer. This overwhelming problem, with our imperfect comprehension of what it involves, we must and can leave with Him. Even in what to us is its hopeless darkness, we know that He is ruling and arranging. "Even so, Father, to what is good in Thy sight."

"All things shall be subject unto Him," not only, as now, in right and actual control, but openly, confessedly, to all and by all, of all classes. The problem of dealing with that subject world, of redeemed as of condemned creatures, is one for His supreme perfection.

INDEX.

Administrator of Baptism, 224.
Agnosticism, 85.
Angelology, 237.
Angels, Creation of, 237 ; Doctrine of, 237 ; Fallen, 240.
Annihilation, 249.
Anthropological Argument for the Existence of God, 81.
Anthropomorphism, 88, 96.
Anthropopathisms, 96.
Apocrypha, 22.
Arguments for the Existence of God, 79, 80, 81.
Articles, On the Church, 220.
Atheism, 83 ; Forms of, 84.
Atonement of Christ, 187.
Atoning Mediation, The, 197 ; Theories of, 198.

Baptism, Manner of, 224 ; Proper Administrator of, 224 ; Sacrament of, 223 ; Subjects of, 225 ; XXVII. Article, on, 226.
Baptismal Regeneration, 227.

Canon of New Testament, 26 ; Muriatorian, 30 ; of Old Testament, 20, 22 ; of Scripture, 19.
Cave, Professor, on Canon of Scripture, 24.
Change, The Spiritual, 211 ; Nature of, 215.
Chastisement, Divine, 170.
Christ, Atonement of, 187 ; a Teacher, 184 ; Example of, 185.
Christ's Resurrection, 193 ; Sufferings, Efficacy of, 184 ; Sufferings Necessary, 186 ; Work in its Application, 202.
Church and Sacraments, 219 ; Visible and Invisible, 219, 220.
Conditional Immortality, Theory of, 249.
Consequences of Sin, 166.
Consubstantiated Presence, 231.
Contingency, Argument from, 79.
Cosmological Argument for the Existence of God, 79.
Creation of Angels, 237 ; of the World, 123 ; not Arrangement, 125.

INDEX.

Deism, Definition of, 86.
Deistic Naturalism, 11.
Demoniacal Possession, 242.
Depravity, Human, 151, 154, 158.
Descartes, 129.
Diatessaron of Tatian, 30.
Difficulties as Regards Omniscience, 100.
Divine Attributes, 87; Unity, 90.
Doctrine of Angels, 237; God, 74; Man, 135; Sin, 149; Trinity, 113.

Eden, The Test of, 142.
Efficacy of Christ's Sufferings, 184.
Election and Foreordination, 101.
Endless Punishment, 248.
Eschatology, 245.
Eternity of God, 95
Eusebius, Canon of New Testament, 31.
Evil, Origin of, 142.
Evolution, 127.
Exaltation, Heavenly, 204, 207.
Existence of God, Arguments for, 79, 80, 81; Proofs of, 76.

Faith, 205.
Fall of Man, 141, 147.
Final Judgment, 246, 247; Perseverance, 217; Resurrection, 246, 247.
Foreknowledge not Foreordination, 101.
Foreordination and Election, 101.

God, Doctrine of, 74; Eternity of, 95; How Known, 11; Moral Attributes of, 104; Omnipotence of, 97; Omnipresence of, 103; Omniscience of, 98; Proofs of Existence of, 76; Revealed in His Works, 12; Scriptural Statements of, 75; Spirituality of, 93; Wisdom of, 108.
Government, Divine, 131.
Governmental Theory of Mediation, 199.

Henotheism, 93.
Hodge, Definition of Inspiration, 54.
Holiness of God, 105.
Holy Ghost, Deity of, 119; Personality of, 119; Sin Against, 164.
Human Personality, The Analogy of the Divine, 88.

Ignorance, Sins of, 162.
Image of God, Man Made in, 135.
Immortality, Theory of Conditional, 249.

Inspiration, Definitions of, 54 ; Evidences of, 35 ; Objections to, 55 ; of Scripture, 34 ; of the Old Testament, 41 ; Theories of, 47.
Intercession of Christ, 194.
Invisible Church, 220.
Irenæus of Lyons, 29.
Irresistible Grace, 216.

Josephus, 20.
Judgment, Final, 246, 247.
Judicial Theory of Mediation, 198.
Justice of God, 107.
Justification, 202.
Justin Martyr, 22, 29.

Knapp, Definition of Depravity, 159 ; Definition of Inspiration, 54.

Lay Baptism, 225.
Lord's Supper, The Articles on the, 234 ; Ecclesiastically Defined, 235 ; Real Presence in, 232 ; Sacrament of, 228 ; Sacrifice in the, 229.
Love, Divine Attribute of, 110.

Man, Primeval Condition of, 135.
Manifestation of Christ as Saviour, 180.
Martineau, on the Idea of God, 74.
Matheson, Dr., Quoted, 92.
Mediation, The Atoning, 197.
Miracles, 69 ; Naturalistic Explanations of, 73 ; Not necessarily Contradictory to Natural Law, 134 ; Objections to, 72 ; Scriptural Words Descriptive of, 71.
Moral Attributes of God, 104.
Muriatorian Canon, 30.
Mystery, 64 ; Three Senses of Word, 65.

Natural Theology, 13, 14.
Necessity of Revelation, 13.
New Testament, Canon of, 26.
Norton, Professor, Estimate of Copies of Gospels, 33.

Objections to Inspiration, 55 ; to Miracles, 72.
Omnipotence of God, 97.
Omnipresence of God, 103.
Omniscience of God, 98.
Origen, Canon of the New Testament, 30.
Origin of Evil, 142.
Original Sin, Theories of, 155, 156.

Pantheism, 84.
Park, Professor, Definition of Inspiration, 54.
Paternal View of Mediation, 200.
Personality of God, 89; of the Holy Ghost, 119; of Tempter in Eden, 145.
Philo, 20.
Philosophy of Religion, 9.
Polytheism, 91.
Positivism, 85.
Possession, Demoniacal, 242.
Predestination, 216.
Presence in the Lord's Supper, 231.
Preservation, Divine, 128.
Primitive Revelation, Possibility of, 139.
Probation, Future, 173.
Problem of Punishment, 250.
Progress of the Race, 85.
Proofs of Revelation, 66.
Providence, Divine, 130.
Provision of Christ's Work in their Reception, 204.
Punishment, Divine, 169; Endless, 248; Positive, 173; Problem of, 250.

Race, Unity of the, 138.
Real Presence, 232.
Reason as Related to Revelation, 15.
Regeneration in Baptism, 22.
Religion, Definition of, 4; Difference with Theology, 4; New Testament Names of, 5; Science of, 6.
Repentance, Expiative Effects of, 178.
Restorationism, 249.
Resurrection, Final, 246, 247; of Christ, 193.
Revelation a Necessity, 13, 14; Evidence in, of the Existence of God, 82; Human Capacity for, 14; Relation of Reason to, 15; Proofs of, 66.
Righteousness of God, 107.

Sacrament of Baptism, 223; of the Lord's Supper, 228.
Sacraments, Christian, 222.
Sacrifice in the Lord's Supper, 229.
Sacrifices for Sin, 176.
Salvation from Sin, 176; Work of the Spirit in, 200.
Sanday, Professor, on Inspiration, 59.
Sanctification, 203, 206.

Satan, 241.
Science and Secondary Causes, 9 ; and Theology, 7, 8.
Scriptural Proof of the Atonement, 188 ; Divine Unity, 90 ; Doctrine of Trinity, 116 ; Eternity of God, 96 ; Omnipresence of God, 103 ; Spirituality of God, 94.
Sin, Actual, 160 ; Against the Holy Ghost, 164 ; Doctrine of, 149 ; in its Consequences, 166 ; Inward Effects of, 168 ; Original, 150 ; Salvation from, 176 ; Various Degrees in, 161.
Sins of Omission and Commission, 161.
Smith, Dean, on Creation, 125.
Son, Deity of the, 118.
Son of God, Christ the, 181.
Son of Man, Christ the, 180.
Sources of Theological Truth, 11.
Sparrow, Dr., on Omnipotence of God, 97.
Specific Revelation, 13.
Spinoza, Pantheism of, 84.
Spirit, Blessed, in Work of Salvation, 209.
Spiritual Change, 211 ; Nature of, 215.
Spirituality of God, 93.
Subjects of Baptism, 225.
Substantiated Presence, 231.

Talmud, 21, 23.
Tatian, Diatessaron of, 30.
Teleological Argument for the Existence of God, 80.
Temptation in Eden, 143.
Tempter in Eden, Personality of, 145.
Test of Eden, The, 142.
Theism, Definition of, 86.
Theology, Conflict with Science, 7, 8 ; Definitions of, 2, 3, 10 ; Difference with Religion, 4 ; Relation to Science, 7 ; Sources of Material for, 3.
Theory of Conditional Immortality, 249.
Theories of Inspiration, 47 ; Mediation, 198 ; Original Sin, 155, 156.
Total Depravity, 159.
Tradition, Authority of, 61.
Traditionalist, Definition of, 63.
Transgression, First, 141.
Transubstantiated Presence, 231.
Trinity, Doctrine of, 113 ; Human Analogies of, 114 ; Scriptural Proof of, 116.
Truth of God, 106.

Ultimate Cause, 9.
Unbelief as to the Divine Existence, 83.
Unity, Divine, 90; of the Race, 138.
Universalism, 249.

Whately, Archbishop, on the Trinity, 121.
Wisdom of God, 108.
World, Creation of, 123.

www.ingramcontent.com/pod-product-compliance
Lightning Source LLC
Chambersburg PA
CBHW032149230426
43672CB00011B/2496